Wrestling with God

Wrestling with God

Finding Hope and Meaning in
Our Daily Struggles to Be Human

Ronald Rolheiser

IMAGE
NEW YORK

IMAGE is a registered trademark and the "I" colophon is
a trademark of Penguin Random House LLC.

Grateful acknowledgment is made to the following for permission to reprint
the previously published material: "Covenant" by Margaret Halaska, OSF
(*Review for Religious*, May/June 1981, Saint Louis University Libraries).
Reprinted by permission of Jesuit Archives and Research Center.

Library of Congress Cataloging-in-Publication Data
is available upon request.

ISBN 978-0-8041-3945-8
Ebook ISBN 978-0-8041-3946-5

PRINTED IN THE UNITED STATES OF AMERICA

Book design by Andrea Lau
Jacket design by Alane Gianetti
Jacket photography by Mari Owen/Arcangel

1 3 5 7 9 10 8 6 4 2

First Edition

For all of you who are struggling
with God, faith, and religion in your lives.
May this book honor your questions,
your resistance, your longing, and your honesty.

The struggle between God and humans breaks out in everyone, together with the longing for reconciliation. Most often this struggle is unconscious and short-lived. . . . The stronger the soul and the flesh, the more fruitful the struggle and the richer the final harmony. God does not love weak souls and flabby flesh. The spirit wants to have to wrestle with flesh which is strong and full of resistance.

—NIKOS KAZANTZAKIS,
The Last Temptation of Christ

CONTENTS

PREFACE

13

CHAPTER ONE

Wrestling for Self-Understanding
Within a Complex Nature

19

CHAPTER TWO

Wrestling with Our Erotic Energies

45

CHAPTER THREE

Wrestling with Fear

63

CHAPTER FOUR

Wrestling with the Gospel Mandate
to Reach Out to the Poor

79

CHAPTER FIVE

Wrestling with Faith and Doubt

99

CHAPTER SIX

Wrestling with God

127

CHAPTER SEVEN

Wrestling for Faith Within a Complex Culture

157

CHAPTER EIGHT

Some Guidelines for the Long Haul

175

ACKNOWLEDGMENTS

197

Wrestling with God

PREFACE

In 1970 Alvin Toffler wrote a book called *Future Shock*, in which he argued that a person born in the year 1900 who lived until 1970 would see more changes in his or her life than someone who had lived through the previous nineteen hundred years. Hard to believe, but no doubt true.

But Toffler wrote that book nearly fifty years ago. The last few decades have brought about changes in our lives that we could not even have imagined in the 1970s. The Internet and an ever-exploding information technology have put a smartphone or a computer into the hands of almost everyone on this planet. Thousands of television channels and more than a billion websites bring the whole world to our living rooms and bedrooms. Globalization has reshaped virtually all of our communities in terms of ethnicity, culture, and religion. The ever-evolving sexual revolution has radically altered how our world sees love, commitment, marriage, and family. Political and religious extremism polarizes our communities and countries and encourages us to live in fear. Both faith and church attendance have fallen sharply in the last eighty years, leaving more people uncertain about what they believe in and fewer people walking through church doors.

We are like pioneers settling a new world nobody has lived in before. Our task, of course, is not just to survive, but to somehow thrive, flourish, and find meaning, happiness, and, not least, faith—something to believe in and to commit ourselves to in a world where nothing seems solid or permanent.

This quest sets before us a whole range of new challenges in terms of how we understand life, love, sexuality, family, country, religion, faith, and God. Traditionally, people looked to their churches for guidance on how to meet new challenges. Today, for all kinds of reasons, both good and bad, fewer people are turning to religion for answers. A certain distrust of churches seems to be part of our cultural ethos, and so more people are leaning on their own instincts and resources to sort through life's big questions.

For the most part this search is honest, but seeking the road of faith and meaning without the classical road maps is fraught with almost insurmountable obstacles, namely, a culture that too easily surrenders to personal comfort, narcissism, greed, grandiosity, paranoia, fear, exclusivity, bitterness, unforgiveness, superficiality, pseudosophisti-

Sexton once called that "gnawing pestilential rat" inside us. Our deepest desire is a gnawing disquiet inside us, a longing for Someone big enough to embrace our questions and hold our doubts.

RONALD ROLHEISER

SAN ANTONIO, TEXAS

AUGUST 1, 2017

✺

CHAPTER ONE

Wrestling for Self-Understanding Within a Complex Nature

I was born into this world with a tortured sensitivity.
For long I have puzzled over the causes of
my psychological anguish.

—RUTH BURROWS

Struggling with Our Own Complexity

In *Telling the Truth*, renowned American theologian Frederick Buechner challenges all spiritual writers to speak with "awful honesty" about the human struggle, even inside the context of faith. Don't sugarcoat things, he warns:

Let the preacher tell the truth. Let him make audible the silence of the news of the world with the sound turned off so that in that silence we can hear the tragic truth of the Gospel which is that the world where God is absent is a dark and echoing emptiness; and the comic truth of the Gospel, which is that it is into the depth of this absence that God makes himself present in such unlikely ways and in such unlikely people that old Sarah and Abraham and maybe when the time comes even Pilate and Job . . . and you and I laugh till the tears run down our cheeks. And finally let him preach this overwhelming of tragedy by comedy, of darkness by light, of the ordinary by the extraordinary, as the tale that is too good not to be true because to dismiss it as untrue is to dismiss along with it the catch of the breath, the beat and lifting of the heart near to or even accompanied by tears, which I believe is the deepest intuition of truth that we have.

Reading this, I was reminded of some of the preaching in my own parish when I was a young boy. I grew up in a small, sheltered, immigrant farming community in the heart of the Canadian prairies. Our parish priests, though wonderfully sincere men, tended to preach to us as if we were a group of idyllic families in the TV series *Little House on the Prairie*. They would share with us how pleased they were to be ministering to simple farm folk living uncomplicated lives, far from the problems of those who were living in the big cities.

Even as a sheltered young boy, I didn't always digest this simplistic concept very well. First of all, I didn't feel very uncomplicated and simple. I harbored a deep restlessness and had more than my own share of heartaches. I already felt then, just as I feel now, that both human life and the human heart have a depth that's always partially beyond our grasp. Also, wonderful as our community was, it had its share of breakdowns, suicides, and interpersonal tensions. On the outside, we sometimes did look like carefree characters living in little houses on the prairies, but deeper things were always brewing underneath. No one is spared both the wondrous mystery and the confusing pathos of life's complexity.

Good art is good precisely because it takes that complexity seriously and shines a light on it in a way that doesn't resolve the tension too easily. Poor art is invariably sentimental precisely because it does not take that complexity seriously, either by refusing to acknowledge it or by resolving it too easily.

The same holds true for good spirituality. It needs to take seriously the complexity of the human heart. Thomas Aquinas once posed the question, What is the adequate object of the human intellect and will? In contemporary terms, he is asking, What would completely satisfy our every aching and longing? His answer: all being, everything, all that is. We would have to know and somehow be affectively connected to "everything, all that is" for our restless minds and hearts to come to full peace. Because that is impossible in this life, we shouldn't be naive as to how habitually restless and complex our lives are going to be.

Perhaps the most popular spiritual writer in the last half century has been Henri Nouwen, and the great gift of his writings is that they introduce us to the complexity of our own lives and give us permission to understand that such complexity is normal. We aren't necessarily overgreedy, oversexed, or overrestless. We are just normal, complicated human beings walking around in human skin. That's what real life feels like! This is also a clear truth inside the scriptures and the Gospels. The scriptures are filled with stories of persons finding God and helping bring about God's kingdom, even as their own lives are often fraught with mess, confusion, frustration, betrayal, infidelity, and sin. There are no simple human beings immune to the spiritual, psychological, sexual, and relational complexities that beset us all.

And in the end, that's a good thing: our complex nature among other things keeps us forever aware, despite our own fear and sloth, that the mystery of life is infinitely bigger than what we are comfortable with most of the time. Our pathological complexity presses us toward ever greater light.

An awareness and an acceptance of the pathological complexity of our own lives can be the place where we finally find the threads of empathy and forgiveness: Life is difficult for everybody. Everyone is hurting. We don't need to blame anyone. We are all beset with the same issues. Understanding and accepting that truth can help us to forgive each other—and then forgive ourselves.

Fire and Glue—The Human Soul's Innate Tension

"What does it profit you if you gain the whole world but suffer the loss of your own soul?"

We generally don't grasp the full range of Jesus's meaning in this scripture. We tend to interpret his words this way: What good is it if someone gains riches, fame, pleasure, and glory and then dies and goes to hell? What good is earthly glory or pleasure if we miss out on eternal life?

Well, at the end of the day, that meaning is valid, but it isn't the main point he is making; instead, he is making a point about our health and happiness here and now, in this life. To understand Jesus's words, we need to consider what it means "to lose your soul" in this life, before death.

What is a soul, and how can it be lost? Since a soul is immaterial and spiritual, it cannot be pictured. We have to use abstract terms to try to understand it. Going back to Aristotle, philosophers have tended to define the soul as a double principle inside every living being: for them, the soul is both *the principle of life and energy* inside us as well as *the principle of integration*. In essence, the soul is two things: it's the fire inside us giving us life and energy, and it's the glue that holds us together. While that definition sounds abstract, it's anything but that, because we have firsthand experience of what this means.

If you have ever been at the bedside of a dying person, you know exactly when the soul leaves the body. You know the precise moment, not because you see something float away from the body, but because one minute you see a person, whatever her struggle and agony, with energy, fire, tension in her body, and a minute later that body is completely inert, devoid of all energy and life. Nothing animates it anymore. It becomes a corpse. However aged or diseased that body might be, until the second of death it is still one integrated organism. But at the very second of death that body ceases to be one organism and becomes instead a series of chemicals that now begin to separate and go their own ways. Once the soul is gone, so too are all life and integration. The body no longer contains any energy, and it's no longer glued together.

And since the soul is a double principle, doing two

things for us, there are two corresponding ways of losing our souls. Our vitality and energy can die or we can become unglued and fall apart—petrification or dissipation—in either case we lose our souls.

If that is true, then this very much nuances the question of how we should care for our souls. What is healthy food for our souls? For instance, if I am watching television on a given night, what's good for my soul? Religious programming? A football game? A mindless sitcom? A nature program? Some iconoclastic talk show?

What's healthy for my soul? is a legitimate question, but a trick one at the same time. Because we lose our soul in opposite ways, care of the soul is a refined alchemy that has to determine when to heat things up and when to cool things down. What's healthy for my soul on a given night depends a lot upon what I'm struggling with more: Am I losing my soul because I'm losing vitality, energy, hope, and graciousness in my life? Am I growing bitter, rigid, sterile, becoming a person who's painful to be around? Or, conversely, am I full of life and energy but so full of it that I am falling apart, dissipating, losing my sense of self? Am I petrifying or dissipating? Both states are a loss of soul. A petrifying soul needs more fire, something to rekindle its energy. A dissipating soul already has too much fire; it needs some cooling down and some glue.

This tension between the principle of energy and the principle of integration within the human soul is also one of the great archetypal tensions between liberals and conservatives. In terms of an oversimplification, but a useful one, it's true to say that liberals tend to protect and promote the energy principle, the fire, while conservatives tend to protect and promote the integration principle, the glue. Both are right, both are needed, and both need to respect the other's instinct, because the soul is a double principle and both of them need protection.

After we die we can go to heaven or hell. That's one way of speaking about losing or saving our souls. But Christian theology also teaches that heaven and hell start in this life. We can weaken or destroy the God-given life inside us in the present time. We can lose our souls either by not having enough fire or by not having enough glue.

The Deep Roots of Our Inner Complexities

We live in a world where just about everything overstimulates our grandiosity, even as we are handed fewer tools to deal with that affliction.

We all nurse a deep, irrepressible sense that we are singularly special and destined for greatness. This condition besets all seven billion of us on this planet. Simply put, each of us cannot help but feel that he or she is the center of the universe. This makes for a scary situation, because this delusion is mostly unacknowledged, and we are generally ill-equipped to deal with it. It's a recipe for jealousy and conflict, not peace and harmony.

And yet this condition isn't our fault, nor is it in itself a moral flaw in our nature. Our grandiosity comes from the way God made us. We are made in the image and likeness of God. This is the most fundamental, dogmatic truth inside the Judeo-Christian understanding of the human person. However, it is not to be conceived of simplistically, as some beautiful icon stamped inside our souls. Rather, it needs to be conceived of in this way: God is fire, infinite fire, an energy that is relentlessly seeking to embrace and infuse all of creation. And that fire is inside us, creating in us a feeling of godliness, an intuition that we too have divine energies, and a pressure to be singularly special and to achieve some form of greatness.

In a manner of speaking, to be made in the image and likeness of God is to have a microchip of divinity inside us. This constitutes our greatest dignity but also creates our biggest problems. The infinite does not sit calmly inside the finite. Because we have divine energy inside us we do not make easy peace with this world; our longings and desires are too grandiose. Not only do we live in that perpetual disquiet that Saint Augustine highlighted in his much-quoted dictum "You have made us for yourself, Lord, and our hearts are restless until they rest in you!" but this innate grandiosity has us forever nursing the belief that we are special, uniquely destined, and born to somehow stand out and be recognized and acknowledged for our specialness.

As a result, all of us are driven outward by a divine gene to somehow make a statement with our lives, to somehow create a personal immortality, and to somehow give birth to some artifact of specialness that the whole world has to take note of. This isn't an abstract concept; it's utterly earthy. The evidence for it is seen in every newscast, bombing, and daredevil stunt—any situation where someone seeks to stand out. It's also seen in the universal hunger for fame, the longing to be known, and the need to be recognized as unique and special.

But this grandiosity, in and of itself, isn't our fault, nor is it necessarily a moral flaw. It comes from the way we are made, ironically from what is highest and best in us. The problem today is that we live in a world in which our grandiosity is being overstimulated—a condition that is not being recognized—and we usually aren't given the religious and psychological tools to grapple with it generatively. What are these tools?

Psychologically, we need images of the human person that allow us to understand ourselves in a healthy way but also include an acceptance of our limitations, our frustrations, our anonymity, and the fact that our lives must make gracious space for everyone else's life. We need better psychological tools for handling our grandiosity: to understand our own life, admittedly as unique and special, but still as one life among millions of other unique and special lives.

Religiously, our faith and our churches need to offer us an understanding of the human person that gives us the insights and the disciplines (discipleship) to enable us to live out our uniqueness and our specialness, even as we make peace with our own mortality, our limitations, our frustrations, our anonymity, and create space for the uniqueness and specialness of everyone else's life. In essence, religion has to give us the tools to access the divine fire inside us and act on the talents and gifts God has graced us with in a healthy way, but with the concomitant discipline to humbly acknowledge that these gifts are not our own, that they come from God, and that all we are and achieve is God's grace. Only then will we not be killed by failure and inflated by success.

The task in life, the poet Robert Lax suggests, is not so much finding a path in the woods as of finding a rhythm to walk in.

Our Nature and God's Intent—
at Odds with Each Other?

An American humorist was once asked what he loved most in life. This was his reply: *I love women best, music and science next, whiskey next, God fourth, and my fellowman hardly at all!*

This ranking flashed through my mind recently when I was giving a lecture and a woman asked, Why did God build us in one way and then almost all of the time expect us to act in a way contrary to our instincts? I knew what she meant. Our natural instincts and spontaneous desires generally seem at odds with that toward which they are supposedly directed—namely, God and eternal life. A religious perspective, it would seem, calls us to reverse the order described by the American humorist; that is, we should love God first, our neighbor just as deeply, and then accord to the human pleasures we are so naturally drawn to a very subordinate role. But that's not what happens most of the time. Generally, we are drawn, and drawn very powerfully, toward the things of this earth: other people, pleasure, beautiful objects, sex, money, comfort. These seemingly have a more powerful grip on us than do the things of faith and religion.

Doesn't this put our natural feelings at odds with how God intended us to feel and act? Why do we seem to be built in one way and then called to live in another way?

The question is a good one and, unfortunately, is often answered in a manner that merely deepens the quandary. Often we are simply told that *we shouldn't feel this way*, that not putting God and religious things first in our feelings is a religious and moral fault, as if our natural wiring were somehow all wrong and we were responsible for its flaw. But that answer is both simplistic and harmful: it misunderstands God's design, guilt-trips us, and leaves us feeling bipolar vis-à-vis our natural makeup and the demands of faith.

How do we reconcile the seeming incongruity between our natural makeup and God's intent for us?

We need to understand human instinct and human desire at a deeper level. We might begin with Saint Augustine's memorable maxim *You have made us for yourself, Lord, and our hearts are restless until they rest in you!* When we analyze our natural makeup, natural instincts, and natural desires more deeply, we see that all of these ultimately are drawing us beyond the more immediate objects and pleasures with which they appear to be obsessed. They are drawing us, persistently and unceasingly, toward God.

Karl Rahner, one of the foremost theologians of the twentieth century, in trying to explain this, makes a distinction between what we desire *explicitly* and what we desire *implicitly*. Our instincts and natural desires draw us toward various explicit things—love for another person, friendship, a work of art or music, a vacation, a movie, a good meal, a sexual encounter, an achievement that brings us honor, a sporting event, and countless others—that, on the surface at least, would seem to have nothing to do with God and are drawing our attention away from God. But, as Rahner shows, and as is evident in our experience, in every one of those explicit desires there is present, implicitly, beneath the desire and as the deepest part of that desire, the longing for and pursuit of something more profound. Ultimately, we are longing for the depth that grounds every person and object: God. To cite one of Rahner's more graphic examples, a man obsessed with sexual desire who seeks out a prostitute is, implicitly, seeking the bread of life, irrespective of his crass surface intent.

God didn't make a mistake in designing human desire. God's intent is written into the very DNA of desire. Ultimately, our makeup directs us toward God, no matter how obsessive, earthy, lustful, and pagan a given desire might appear on a given day. Human nature is not at odds with the call of faith, not at all.

Moreover, those powerful instincts within our nature, which can seem so selfish and amoral at times, have their own moral intelligence and purpose: they protect us, make us reach out for what keeps us alive, and, not least, ensure that the human race keeps perpetuating itself. Finally, God also put those earthy instincts in us to pressure us to enjoy life and taste its pleasures—while like a loving old grandparent watching his children at play, God remains happy just to see his children's delight in the moment, knowing that there will be time enough ahead when pain and frustration will force those desires to focus on deeper things.

When we analyze in more depth God's design for human nature and understand ourselves more deeply within that design, we realize that, at a level deeper than spontaneous feeling, and at a level deeper than the wisecracks we make about ourselves, we in fact do love God best; love our neighbor quite a bit; and, very happily, love whiskey and the pleasures of life quite a bit as well.

Our Perpetual Disquiet

What is the real root of human loneliness? A flaw within our makeup? Inadequacy and sin? Or does Saint Augustine's adage *You have made us for yourself, Lord, and our hearts are restless until they rest in you!* say it all?

Saint Augustine's words are not quite enough. We are infinite souls inside finite lives and that alone should be enough to explain our incessant and insatiable aching, but there is something else: our souls enter the world bearing the brand of eternity and this gives all of our aching a particularized coloring.

How do we explain this? The much-esteemed theologian and philosopher Bernard Lonergan suggests that the human soul does not come into the world as a tabula rasa, a pure, clean sheet of paper onto which anything can be written. Rather, for him, *we are born with the brand of the first principles indelibly stamped inside our souls.* What does he mean by this?

Classical theology and philosophy name four transcendental qualities that are somehow true of everything that exists: *oneness, truth, goodness,* and *beauty.* Everything that exists somehow bears these four qualities; however, these qualities are perfect only inside God. God alone is perfect oneness, perfect truth, perfect goodness, and perfect beauty. Lonergan asserts that God brands these four qualities, in their perfection, into the core of the human soul.

Hence we come into the world already knowing, however dimly, perfect oneness, perfect truth, perfect goodness, and perfect beauty because they already lie inside us like an inerasable brand. Thus we can tell right from wrong because we already know perfect truth and goodness in the core of our souls, just as we also instinctively recognize love and beauty because we already know them in a perfect way, however darkly, inside ourselves. In this life, we don't learn truth, we recognize it; we don't learn love, we recognize it; and we don't learn what is good, we recognize it. We recognize these qualities because we already possess them in the core of our souls.

Some mystics taught that the human soul comes from God and that the last thing God does before putting a soul into a body is to kiss the soul. The soul then goes through life always dimly remembering that kiss, a kiss of perfect love, and the soul measures all of life's loves and kisses against that primordial perfect kiss.

The Ancient Greek Stoics taught something similar: Souls preexisted inside God, and before putting a soul into a body, God would blot out the memory of its preexistence. But the soul would always be unconsciously drawn toward

God, because, having come from God, it would always dimly remember its real home and ache to return there.

In one rather interesting version of this notion, the Ancient Greek Stoics taught that God put a soul into a body only when a baby was already fully formed in its mother's womb. Immediately after putting the soul into the body, God would seal off the memory of its preexistence by physically shutting the baby's lips against its ever speaking about it. That's why we have a little cleft under our noses, just above the center of our lips, where God's finger sealed our lips. That is why whenever we are struggling to remember something, our index finger instinctually rises to that cleft under our nose—we are trying to retrieve a primordial memory.

Perhaps a metaphor will be helpful here: We commonly speak of things as "ringing true" or "ringing false." Is there a bell inside us that somehow rings in a certain way when things are true and in another when they are false? In essence, yes! We nurse an unconscious memory of once having known love, goodness, and beauty perfectly. Things will therefore ring true or false, depending upon whether or not they are measuring up to the love, goodness, and beauty that already reside in a perfect form at the core of our souls.

And that core, that center, that place in our souls where we have been branded with the first principles and where we unconsciously remember the kiss of God before we were born, is the real seat of that congenital ache inside us, which, in this life, can never be fully assuaged. We bear the dark memory, as Henri Nouwen says, of once having been caressed by hands far gentler than we ever meet in this life.

Our souls dimly remember having once known perfect love and perfect beauty. But, in this life, we never quite encounter that perfection, even as we forever ache for someone or something to meet us at that depth. This creates in us a moral loneliness, a longing for what we term a *soul mate*—namely, someone who can genuinely recognize, share, and respect what lies at the depth of our souls.

Both Angel and Mammal

Two decades ago, Hollywood made a movie called *City of Angels*. It is the story of Seth, an angel whose job it is to accompany the spirits of the recently deceased to the afterlife. On one such mission, while waiting in a hospital, he falls in love with a brilliant young woman who is a surgeon. Because he is an angel, Seth has never experienced the human senses and now, deeply in love, he longs to physically touch and make love to his beloved. But he faces a dilemma: as an angel with free will he has the option to relinquish his angelic status and become a human, but only at the cost of renouncing his present immortality.

It's a tough choice: immortality without sensual experience versus sensual experience accompanied by all the contingencies that earthly mortality brings—diminishment, aging, sickness, eventual death. He chooses the latter, renouncing his immortal status for the pleasures of earthly senses.

The vast majority of people watching this movie, I suspect, will laud his choice. Everything in our hearts moves us to believe that it's cold and inhuman to choose otherwise. The overpowering reality of the senses, especially when we are in love, can make everything else seem unreal, ethereal, and second-best. What we experience through our senses, what we see, hear, taste, touch, and smell, is what's real for us. We have our own version of Descartes's well-known philosophic proposition: "I think, therefore I am." For us, the ultimate thing that cannot be doubted is "I feel, therefore I am!"

In virtually every major religious tradition, spirituality, at least in its popular conception, seems to take the opposite position. Spirit has classically (and sometimes almost dogmatically) been affirmed as above the senses, a needed guard against them, on a higher plane, superior. Sensual pleasure, although occasionally honored in the realm of aesthetics, was perennially denigrated as furtive, superficial, and a hindrance to the spiritual life. We took Saint Paul's admonition that the "flesh lusts against the spirit" in the Greek, dualistic sense of "body is bad and spirit is good."

Today, in the secularized world, the opposite seems true. The senses resoundingly trump the spirit. Secularized angels, unlike the religious angels of old, make the same choice as Seth. The seeming vagueness of the spirit is no match for the reality of the senses.

So which is more real?

At the end of the day, it's a false dichotomy. Our senses and our spirit both offer life, both are very important, and neither operates without the other.

As Christians, we believe that we are both—body and soul, flesh and spirit—and that neither can be separated from the other. In our search for life, meaning, happiness, and God, we should not forget that our spirit is open to life only through our senses, and our senses provide depth and meaning only because they are animated by spirit.

The poet W. H. Auden once wrote, "All of us know the few things Man as a mammal can do." But we're not just mammal, we're equal part angel, and once we add that to the equation, the very limited joys that mammals can enjoy (animal pleasures) can become unlimited joys for us as humans and transform what we can experience in love, friendship, altruism, aesthetics, sexuality, mysticism, food, drink, and humor. Our senses make these real, even as our spirit gives them meaning.

And so a healthy spirituality needs to honor both the senses and the spirit. The ordinary pleasures of life can be deep or shallow, more mystical or more mammal, depending upon how much we honor what's spirit and what's angel within us. Conversely, our spirituality and our prayer lives can be real or more of a fantasy, depending upon how much we incarnate them in what's sensual and what's mammal within us.

This holds true in every realm of our lives. For example, sexuality can be deep or shallow, more mystical or more mammal, contingent upon how much of it is soulful and how much of it is merely sensual; in the same way, it can be disembodied, sterile, and merely fantasy if it is all soul and no body. The same is true of our experience of beauty: any sensual experience—seeing, hearing, touching, tasting, or smelling—can be deep or shallow, depending upon how much soul is in it, just as any experience of beauty can seem unreal and imaginary if it is too divorced from the senses.

Some years ago, I was attending a seminar in anthropology. At one point, the lecturer said, "What psychology and spirituality keep forgetting is that we are mammals." As a theologian and spiritual writer (and celibate) I was hit hard by the truth of his words. He's right! How easily we forget this inside our churches. But our churches are right too in consistently reminding us that we are also angels.

Poor Seth, the tormented angel: he shouldn't have had to make that choice. Neither should we.

Torn Between the Sacred and the Secular

"Because, my God, though I lack the soul-zeal and the sublime integrity of your saints, I yet have received from you an overwhelming sympathy for all that stirs within the dark mass of matter; because I know myself to be irremediably less a child of heaven than a son of earth."

The philosopher Pierre Teilhard de Chardin wrote those words, and like Saint Augustine's famous opening to his *Confessions,* they not only describe a lifelong tension inside their author but also name the foundational pieces for an entire spirituality. For everyone who is emotionally healthy and honest, there will be a lifelong tension between the seductive attractions of this world and the lure of God. The earth, with its beauties, its pleasures, and its physicality, can take our breath away and have us believe that this world is all there is, and that this world is all that needs to be. Who needs anything further? Isn't life here on earth enough? Besides, what proof is there for any reality and meaning beyond our lives here?

But even as we are so powerfully, and rightly, drawn to the world and what it offers, another part of us finds itself also caught in the embrace and grip of another reality, the divine, which though more inchoate is not less unrelenting. It too tells us that it is real, that its reality ultimately offers life, that it also should be honored, and that it also may not be ignored. And, just like the reality of the world, it too presents itself as both promise and threat. Sometimes it feels like a warm cocoon in which we sense ultimate shelter, and sometimes we feel its power as a threatening judgment on our superficiality, mediocrity, and sin. Sometimes it blesses our fixation on earthly life and its pleasures, and sometimes it frightens us and relativizes both our world and our lives. We can push it away by distraction or denial, but it stays, always creating a powerful tension inside us: we are irremediably children of both heaven and earth; both God and the world have a right to our attention.

That's how it's meant to be. God made us irremediably physical, fleshy, and oriented to this world, with virtually every instinct inside us reaching for the things of earth. We shouldn't then expect that God wants us to shun earth, deny its genuine beauty, and step out of our bodies, our natural instincts, and our physicality in order to fix our eyes only on the things of heaven. God did not build this world as a moral testing ground, where our obedience and piety are to be tested against the lure of earthly pleasure, to see if we're worthy of heaven. This world is its own mystery and has its own meaning, a God-given one. It's not simply a stage upon which we, as humans, play out our individual dramas of salvation and then close the curtain. It's a place for all of us—humans, animals, insects, plants, water, rocks, and soil—to enjoy a home together.

But that's the root of a great tension inside us: unless we deny either our most powerful human instincts or our most powerful religious sensibilities we will find ourselves forever torn between two worlds, with seemingly conflicting loyalties, caught between the lure of this world and the lure of God. I know how true this is in my own life. I was born into this world with two incurable loves and have spent my life and ministry caught and torn between the two: I have always loved the pagan world for its honoring of this life and for its celebration of the wonders of the human body and the beauty and pleasure that our five senses bring us. With my pagan brothers and sisters, I too honor the lure of sexuality, the comfort of human community, the delight of humor and irony, and the remarkable gifts given us by the arts and the sciences. But, at the same time, I have always found myself in the grip of another reality: the divine, faith, religion. Its reality too has always commanded my attention—and, more important, dictated the major choices in my life.

My major choices in life incarnate and radiate a great tension because I've tried to be true to a double primordial branding inside me, the pagan and the divine. I can't deny the reality, lure, and goodness of either of them. It's for this reason that I can live as a consecrated, lifelong celibate, doing religious ministry, even as I deeply love the pagan world, bless its pleasures, and bless the goodness of sex, though because of other loyalties, I renounce it. That's also the reason why I chronically apologize to God for the world's pagan resistance, even as I try to make an apologia for God to the world. I've lived with torn loyalties.

That's as it should be. The world is meant to take our breath away, even as we genuflect to the author of that breath.

CHAPTER TWO

Wrestling with Our Erotic Energies

The lusts of the flesh reveal the loneliness of the soul.

—DAG HAMMARSKJÖLD

Sex and Our Culture

As I suggested in my preface, I suspect that no generation in history has experienced as much change as we have undergone in the past two generations. That change is not just in science, technology, medicine, travel, and communications but also in our social infrastructure and our communal ethos. And perhaps nowhere is this change more radical than in the arena of sex. In the past seventy years we have witnessed three major tectonic shifts in how we understand the place of sex in our lives.

First, we moved away from the concept that sex is morally connected to procreation. With few exceptions, prior to 1950, at least in terms of our moral and religious notions, sex was understood as constitutively connected to procreation. This connection wasn't always respected, of course, but it was part of our communal ethos. That association, while still upheld in some of our churches, effectively broke down in our culture about sixty years ago.

The second severing was more radical. Until the 1960s, our culture tied sex to marriage. The norm was that the only moral place for sex was inside a marriage. Again, of course, this wasn't always respected and there was plenty of sex taking place outside marriage. But it wasn't morally or religiously accepted or blessed. People had sex outside marriage, but nobody claimed the practice was right. It was something for which you apologized. The sexual revolution of the 1960s effectively severed that link. Sex, in our cultural understanding, has become an extension of dating, and one of the fruits of that is more people who live together outside marriage and before marriage, without any sense of moral implication. This extramarital coupling has become so prevalent today that sex outside marriage is more the norm than the exception. More young people today will not even have a moral discussion on this topic with either their parents or their churches. Their glib answer: "We don't think like you!" They don't.

But the shift in our sexual ethos didn't stop there. Today we are witnessing, not least on our university campuses, the phenomenon of "hookup" sex, where sex is deliberately and consciously cut off from love, emotion, and commitment. This constitutes the most radical shift of all. As Donna Freitas has documented in *The End of Sex*, more young people are making a conscious decision to delay looking for a marriage partner while they prepare for or launch a career, and while in that hiatus, which might last anywhere from ten to twenty years, they plan to be sexually active, but with that sexual activity consciously cut off from love, emotion, and commitment (all of which are feared as time-demanding, messy, and an impediment to study, work, fun, and freedom). The idea is to eventually tie sex to love and commitment, but first to split it off for some years. Sadly, this ethos has taken root. Of course, as with the other shifts in our understanding of sex, this lack of love and commitment has always existed, to which prostitution and singles bars attest. But, until now, no one has claimed that this detachment is healthy.

What is particularly disturbing is not that there is sex taking place outside its prescribed Christian ground, marriage. Human beings have struggled with sex since the beginning of time. More worrisome is that this severance of love from sex is not only being held up as the norm, but also, among many of our own children, being understood and hailed as moral progress, a liberation from darkness. Moreover, a concomitant understanding, often voiced with some moral smugness, is that anyone still holding the traditional view of sex is in need of moral and psychological enlightenment. Who's judging whom here?

What I am about to say may not make me popular among many of my contemporaries, but I want to state here unequivocally that our culture's severing of the nonnegotiable tie between sex and marriage is just plain wrong. It's also naive.

I once attended a conference on sexuality where the keynote speaker, a renowned theologian, suggested that churches have always been far too uptight about sex. She's right about that. We're still a long ways from integrating sexuality and spirituality in a healthy way. However, she went on to ask, "Why all this anxiety about sex? Who's ever been hurt by it anyway?" A more sober insight might suggest, "Who hasn't been hurt by it?" History is strewn with broken hearts, broken families, broken lives, terminal bitterness, murders, and suicides within which sex is the canker.

Admittedly, our churches have never produced a fully healthy, robust theology and spirituality of sex, though nobody else, secular or religious, has either. However, what Christianity has produced, its traditional morality and ethos, does give a fair and important warning to our culture: Don't be naive about sexual energy. It isn't always as friendly and inconsequential as you think!

We are all powerfully, incurably, and wonderfully sexed; this is part of a conspiracy between God and nature. Sexuality lies right next to our instinct for breathing and it is ever-present in our lives.

Spiritual literature tends to be naive and in denial about the power of sexuality, as if it could be dismissed as some insignificant factor in the spiritual journey, when in fact it cannot be dismissed at all. It will always make itself felt, consciously or unconsciously. Nature is almost cruel in this regard, particularly to the young. It fills youthful bodies with powerful hormones before the emotional and intellectual maturity to properly understand and creatively channel that energy is attained. Nature's cruelty, or anomaly, is that it gives someone an adult body before his or her emotions and intellect mature. A lot of physical and moral dangers are associated with a still-developing child walking around in a fully adult body.

The problem is exacerbated by the fact that young people today reach puberty at an ever lower age and marry later in life. This makes for a situation, which has become almost the norm in many cultures, where a young girl or boy reaches puberty at age eleven or twelve and won't marry for about twenty years. This begs the obvious questions: How can the sexuality of young people be emotionally and morally contained during all those years? Where does that leave them in the struggle to remain faithful to the commandments?

Admittedly, nature has its own angle. Its dominant concern is to get each of us into the gene pool. The powerful hormones it begins pouring into our bodies at adolescence and the myriad ways in which it heats up our emotions all have the same intent: nature wants us to be fruitful and multiply, to replicate and perpetuate ourselves and our own species. And nature is uncompromising on this point: at every level of our being (physical, emotional, psychological, and spiritual) there is sexual pressure to get us into the gene pool. So when you next see a young man or woman strutting his or her sexuality, be both sympathetic and understanding: you were once there, and nature is just trying to get him or her into the gene pool. Such are its ways and such are its propensities, and God is in on the conspiracy.

Of course, getting into the gene pool means much more than physically having children, though that is a deep imperative written everywhere inside us that may be ignored only in the face of some major psychological and moral risks. There are other ways of having children, though nature all on its own does not easily accept that. It wants children in the flesh. But the full bloom of sexuality, generative living, takes on other life-giving forms. We have all heard the slogan *Have a child. Plant a tree. Write a book.* There are different ways to get into the gene pool, and all of us know persons who, while not having children of their own and neither writing a book nor planting a tree, are wonderfully generative women and men. Indeed, the religious vow of celibacy is predicated on that truth. Sexuality also has a powerful spiritual dimension.

But, with that being admitted, we can never be naive about the sheer, blind power of our sexuality. Dealing with its brute and unrelenting pressure lies at the root of many of our deepest psychological and moral struggles. This pressure takes on many guises, but always has the same intent—that is, to open our lives to something bigger than ourselves and to remain cognizant of the fact that intimacy with others, the cosmos, and God is our real goal. It is no great surprise that our sexuality is so grandiose that it would have us want to make love to the whole world. Isn't that our real goal?

Sexuality also wreaks havoc with many people's church lives. It is no secret that today one of the major reasons why many people of all ages are no longer regularly attending their churches somehow has to do with their struggles with sexuality and their perception of how their churches view their situation. My point here is not that the churches should change the commandments regarding sex; rather, they should do a couple of things: First, they should more realistically acknowledge the brute power of sexuality in our lives and integrate sexual complexity more honestly into spirituality. Second, the churches should be far more empathic and pastorally sensitive to the issues that beset people because of their sexuality.

Sexuality is a sacred fire. It takes its origins in God and is everywhere, powerfully present inside creation. Denial is not our friend in this instance.

Our Struggle with Sexual Energy

Christians have always struggled with sex, but everyone else has too. No culture, religious or secular, premodern or modern, postmodern or postreligious, exhibits a truly healthy sexual ethos. All churches and cultures struggle with integrating sexual energy, if not in their creeds about sex, at least in the living out of those creeds. Secular culture looks at the church and accuses it of being uptight and antierotic. This is partly true, but the church might well protest that much of its sexual reticence is rooted in the fact that it is one of the few voices still remaining that are challenging anyone about sexual responsibility. The church could also challenge any culture that claims to have found the key to healthy sexuality to step forward and show the evidence. No culture will take up that claim. Everyone is struggling.

Part of that struggle is the seemingly innate incompatibility between what Charles Taylor, probably the most respected academic commentator on secularity, calls "sexual fulfillment and piety," between "squaring our highest aspirations with an integral respect for the full range of human fulfillments."

In his book *A Secular Age*, Taylor suggests that there is a real tension in trying to combine sexual fulfillment with piety and that this reflects a more general tension between human flourishing in general and dedication to God:

> That this tension should be particularly evident in the sexual domain is readily understandable. Intense and profound sexual fulfillment focuses us powerfully on the exchange within the couple; it strongly attaches us possessively to what is privately shared. . . . It was not for nothing that the early monks and hermits saw sexual renunciation as opening the way to the wider love of God.
>
> Now that there is a tension between fulfillment and piety should not surprise us in a world distorted by sin . . . But we have to avoid turning this into a constitutive incompatibility.

How can we avoid doing that? How can we avoid somehow pitting sexual fulfillment against holiness? How can we be robustly sexual and fully spiritual at one and the same time?

In his book *The Road Is How: A Prairie Pilgrimage Through Nature, Desire, and Soul,* naturalist writer Trevor Herriot suggests that human fulfillment and dedication to God—sex and holiness—can be brought together in a way that properly respects both of them. How? Without using the word that is at once so honored and so maligned, he presents us with an image of what chastity means at its true root. Much like Annie Dillard in her book *Holy the Firm,* Herriot draws a certain concept of chastity out of the rhythms of nature and then presents those rhythms as the paradigm of how we should be relating to nature and to each other. And, for Herriot, those rhythms cast a particularly enlightening beam on how we should be relating sexually.

> These days, we watch truckloads of grain pass by and sense that something in us and in the earth is harmed when food is grown and consumed with little intimacy, care, and respect. The local and slow food movements are showing us that the way we grow, distribute, prepare, and eat food is important for the health of our body-to-earth exchanges. The next step may be to realize that the energy that brings pollen to ovary and grows the grain, once it enters our bodies, also needs to be husbanded. The way we respond to our

desire to merge, connect, and be fruitful—stirrings felt so deeply, but often so shallowly expressed—determines the quality of our body-to-body exchanges. . . .

In a world bathed in industrial and impersonal sex, where real connection and tenderness are rare, will we sense also that something in us and in the earth is being harmed from the same absence of intimacy, care, and respect? Will we learn that any given expression of our erotic energies either connects us to or divides us from the world around us and our souls? We are discovering that we must steward the energies captured by nature in the hydrocarbons or in living plants and animals, and thereby improve the ways we receive the fruits of the earth, but we struggle to see the primary responsibility we bear for the small but cumulatively significant explosions of energy we access and transmit as we respond to our own longings to connect, merge, and be fruitful. Learning how to steward the way we bear fruit ourselves as spiritual/sexual beings with a full set of animal desires and angelic ambitions may be more important to the human journey than we fully understand.

Chastity, as imagined by Charles Taylor, Annie Dillard, and Trevor Herriot, has always been the one thing that properly protects sex, the white dress adorning the bride, the means of "squaring our highest aspirations with an integral respect for the full range of human fulfillments," and, not least, the trusted guideline for how we can access and transmit our sexual energy with intimacy, care, and respect.

Sexual Energy and Our Unfinished Symphony

In the Jewish scriptures there's a story that's unique in its capacity both to shock and to fascinate.

A king, Jephthah, is at war and things are going badly. Praying in desperation, he makes a promise to God that should he win this battle he would, upon returning home, sacrifice on the altar the first person he meets.

Some days God has nothing better to do than to hear such prayers. Jephthah's prayer is granted and he wins the battle, but, upon returning home, he is deeply distressed, because the first person he meets is his own daughter, in the full bloom of youth. He loves her deeply, grieves his foolish vow, and is ready to break it for her sake.

But she asks him to go ahead with it. She accepts death on the altar of sacrifice, except for one thing (in stories that bare the soul there is always "one thing" that complicates the plot). In her case, the one thing is that she will die a virgin, unconsummated, unfulfilled, not having achieved full intimacy, and not having given birth to children. And so she asks her father for time in the desert (forty days, the time it takes the desert to do its work) before she dies, to grieve her virginity, the incompleteness of her life.

Her father grants her wish and she goes into the desert with her companions (themselves virgins) for forty days to bewail that she will die a virgin. After this period of mourning, she returns and is ready to die on the altar of sacrifice.

There's a rather nasty patriarchal character to this story (such were the times) and, of course, we are right to abhor the very idea of human sacrifice, but this particular narrative is not historical and is not meant to be taken literally. It's an archetype, a metaphor, a poetry of the soul within which death and virginity are not meant in their literal sense. What do death and virginity mean in this story?

They're metaphors inside a parable meant to teach a profound truth—namely, all of us, no matter what age or state in life, must at some point mourn what's incomplete and not consummated in our lives.

We are all Jephthah's daughters. In the end, like her, we all die virgins, having lived incomplete lives, not having achieved the intimacy we craved, and having yearned to create a lot more things than we were able to birth. In this life, nobody gets the full symphony. There's a place inside us where we all "bewail our virginity," and this is true too of married people, just as it is of celibates. At some deep level on this side of eternity, we all sleep alone.

We need to mourn this incompleteness in whatever way will assuage our grief. When we fail to do so, we go through life disappointed, dissatisfied with our lives, restless inside our own skins, prone to anger, and forever expecting, unrealistically, that someone or something—a marriage partner, a family, children, a church, a sexual partner, a friend, a career, or an achievement—can take all of our loneliness away, give us the complete symphony, and (metaphorically) consummate our lives so that we aren't virgins anymore.

Of course, that's impossible, only God can do that. Our yearnings and our needs are infinite because we are Grand Canyons without a bottom. For that reason, we all sleep alone, living (as Rahner famously puts it) "in the torment of the insufficiency of everything attainable."

Recognizing and accepting this isn't one of our strengths. Just about everything inside our culture today conspires to keep us from admitting this. No more for us the old *Salve Regina* prayer "To thee do we send up our sighs, mourning and weeping in this valley of tears." Good for past generations, but not for us. The last thing we like to admit to is tears, the helpless frustration of our lives at times, and the incontrovertible fact of our own virginity.

We suffer a lot of restlessness, disappointment, and bitterness because of this. Until, like Jephthah's daughter, we can recognize and admit and honor how we really feel, we will forever be fighting something or somebody—usually those persons and things closest to us.

The daydreams of our youth eventually die, though perhaps as we get older we replay them just to feel bygone sentiments (our own version of "The Way We Were") without any practical hope that they will be realized. Time and disappointment have done their work; we no longer look for our daydreams to come true, and the dreams themselves look pretty flat in the context of our actual lives. But what created those dreams years ago hasn't changed; indeed, a part of us now is even more idealistic, and we ache just as much as we ever did, despite our acceptance that daydreams don't come true.

When that happens, it's time to go into the desert and bewail our virginity. Our capacity for genuine self-sacrifice, it would seem, follows from that.

The Need for an Occasional Visit from the Goddess of Chastity

Ancient Greeks used their myths to express much of their psychological and spiritual wisdom. They didn't intend for these stories to be taken literally or as historical fact; instead, they used them as metaphors and archetypal illustrations of why life is as it is and how people engage life both generatively and destructively.

Many of these myths were centered on gods and goddesses who mirrored virtually every aspect of life, human behavior, and innate human propensity. Moreover, many of these gods and goddesses were far from moral in their behavior, especially in their sexual lives. They had messy affairs with each other and with human beings. However, despite the messiness and amorality of their sexual behavior, one of the positive features inside these myths was that, for ancient Greeks, sex was always somehow connected to the divine. Even temple prostitution was related to accessing the fertility that emanated from the realm of the gods.

Within this pantheon of gods and goddesses was a goddess named Artemis. Most of the other goddesses were sexually promiscuous, but Artemis was chaste and celibate. Her sexual abstinence represented the place and the value of chastity and celibacy. Pictured as a tall, graceful figure, she was attractive sexually, but her beauty was different from the overt, seductive sexuality of goddesses like Aphrodite and Hera. In the figure of Artemis, sex is depicted as an attractive blend of solitude and integrity. She is frequently portrayed as surrounded by members of her own sex or the opposite sex, who appear as friends and intimates but never lovers.

The implication here is that sexual desire can remain healthy and generative despite someone abstaining from sex. Artemis represents a chaste way of being sexual. She tells us that, in the midst of a sexually soaked world, a person can be generative and happy while chaste and even celibate. Perhaps even more important, Artemis shows us that being chaste doesn't make a person antisexual and sterile: sexuality is wider than sex, and sex itself will be richer and more meaningful if it is also connected to chastity. Claiming your solitude and experiencing friendship and other forms of intimacy are not substitutes for sex but one of its rich modalities.

Here is how the psychotherapist Thomas Moore describes Artemis: "Although she is the most virginal of the goddesses, Artemis is not asexual. She embodies a special kind of sexuality where the accent is on individuality, integrity, and solitude." As such, she is a model not just for celibates but also for people who are sexually active. For the latter, Artemis is the cautionary flag that signals, "I want to be taken seriously, with my integrity and independence assured."

According to Moore, whether we are celibate or sexually active, we all "have periods in life or just moments in a day when we need to be alone, disconnected from love and sex, devoted to an interest of our own, withdrawn and remote. [Artemis] tells us that this preference may not be an antisocial rejection of people but simply a deep, positive, even sexual focusing of oneself and one's world."

This mythical goddess teaches us a much-needed lesson for our world today. Our age has turned sex into a soteriology, a doctrine of salvation. In other words, sex isn't perceived as a means toward heaven; it is identified with heaven itself. It's what we're supposed to be living for. One of the consequences of this is that we can no longer blend our adult awareness with chastity or the genuine complexity and richness of sex. Rather, for many of us, chastity and celibacy are seen as a fearful self-protection that leaves a person dry, sterile, moralistic, antierotic, sexually uptight, and on the periphery of life's joys. Tied to this is the notion that all those rich realities so positively highlighted by Artemis (as well as by the classical Christian notion of chastity)—friendship, nonsexual forms of intimacy, nonsexual pleasures, and the need for integrity and fidelity within sex—are merely substitutes for sex, and second-best ones at that, rather than rich modalities of sex itself.

We are psychologically and spiritually impoverished by that notion, and it puts undue pressure on our sexual lives. When sex is asked to carry the primary load in terms of human generativity and happiness, it cannot help but come up short. And we are seeing that in our world today.

Of course, as Christians, we have our own goddesses of chastity: Mary, the mother of Jesus, and many women saints. Shouldn't we draw our spirituality of chastity from these real human women rather than a mythical pagan goddess? Well, for the most part, we do look to Christian models. Moreover, were Artemis actually a real person, I suspect that both the Virgin Mary and all of our revered virgin saints would very much befriend the Greek goddess.

CHAPTER THREE

Wrestling with Fear

Fear is the heartbeat of the powerless.

—COR DE JONGHE

The Power of Fear

We can deal with almost everything except fear.

In *The Taste of Silence*, a very fine book, the late Belgian spiritual writer Bieke Vandekerckhove candidly shares her struggles with the demons that beset her as she confronted a terminal illness at age nineteen. She singled out three particular demons that tormented her as she faced the prospect of death—*sadness, anger,* and *fear*—and suggested that we can more easily cope with the first two than the third.

Sadness can be handled through tears, through grieving. Sadness fills us like a water glass, but a glass can be emptied. Tears can drain sadness of its bite. We have all, no doubt, experienced the release, the catharsis, that can come through tears. Tears can soften the heart and take away the bitterness of sadness, even while its heaviness remains. Sadness, no matter how heavy, has a release valve. So too does anger. Anger can be expressed and its very expression helps release it so that it flows out of us. No doubt too we have also experienced this. The caution, of course, is that in expressing anger and giving it release we need to be careful not to hurt others, which is the ever-present danger when dealing with anger. With anger we have many outlets: We can shout in rage, beat drums, punch a bag, use profanity, physically exercise until we're exhausted, smash some furniture, utter murderous threats, and rage away at countless things. This isn't necessarily rational and some of these things aren't necessarily moral, but they offer some release. We have means to cope with anger.

Fear, on the other hand, has no such release valves. Most often, there's nothing we can do to lighten or release it. Fear paralyses us, and this paralysis is the very thing which robs us of the strength we would need to combat it. We can beat a drum, rage in profanity, or cry tears, but fear remains. Moreover, unlike anger, fear cannot be taken out on someone else, even though we sometimes try, by scapegoating. But, in the end, it doesn't work. The object of our fear doesn't go away simply because we wish it away. Fear can only be suffered. We have to live with it until it recedes on its own. Sometimes, as the Book of Lamentations suggests, all we can do is to put our mouth to the dust and wait. With fear, sometimes all we can do is endure.

What's the lesson in this?

In her memoirs, the Russian poet Anna Akhmatova recounts an encounter she once had with another woman as the two of them waited outside a Russian prison. Both of their husbands had been imprisoned by Stalin and both of them were there to bring letters and packages to their spouses, as were a number of other women. But the bizarre scene was like something out of the existential literature of the absurd. First of all, the women were unsure whether their husbands were even still alive. If they were, would the guards give the letters and packages they were delivering to their loved ones? Without reason, the guards would make the women wait for hours in the snow and cold before collecting their letters and packages; sometimes they wouldn't meet the women at all. Still, every week, despite the absurdity of it, the women would come, wait in the snow, accept this unfairness, do their vigil, and try to get letters and packages to their loved ones in prison. One morning, as they were waiting, seemingly with no end in sight, one of the women recognized Akhmatova and said to her, "Well, you're a poet. Can you tell me what's happening here?" Akhmatova looked at the woman and replied, "Yes, I can!" And then something like a smile passed between them.

Why the smile? Just to be able to name something, no matter how absurd or unfair, no matter how powerless we are to change it, is to be somehow free of it, above it, in some way transcendent. To name something correctly is to partly free ourselves of its dominance. That's why totalitarian regimes fear artists, writers, religious critics, journalists, and prophets. They name things. That's ultimately the function of prophecy. Prophets don't foretell the future; they properly name the present. Renowned spiritual writer Richard Rohr is fond of saying, "Not everything can be fixed or cured, but it should be named properly." The late psychologist James Hillman has his own way of casting this. He suggests "a symptom suffers most when it doesn't know where it belongs."

Fear can render us impotent. But naming it properly, recognizing where that symptom belongs and how powerless it leaves us, can help us to live with it, without sadness and anger.

Religious Fears

Unless you are already a full saint or a mystic, you will always live with some fear of death and the afterlife. That's simply part of being human. But we can, and must, move beyond our fear of God.

As a child, I lived with a lot of fear. I had a very active imagination and too frequently imagined murderers under my bed, poisonous snakes slithering up my leg, deadly germs in my food, playground bullies looking for a victim, a hundred ways in which I could meet an accidental death, and threats of every kind lurking in the dark. As a child, I was often afraid: afraid of the dark, afraid of death, afraid of the afterlife, and afraid of God.

As I matured, so too did my imagination; it no longer pictured snakes hiding everywhere or murderers under my bed. I began to feel strong, in control, imagining the unknown, with its dark corners, more as an opportunity for growth than as a threat to life. But it was one thing to block out fear of snakes, murderers, and the dark. Not so easily did I overcome my fear of death, fear of the afterlife, and fear of God. These fears are the last demons to be exorcised, and that exorcism is never final, never completely done with. Jesus himself trembled in fear before death, before the unknown that faces us in death. But he didn't tremble in fear before God—the opposite in fact. As he faced death and the unknown, he was able to give himself over to God, in childlike trust, like an infant clinging to a loving parent, and that gave him the strength and courage to undergo an anonymous, lonely, and misunderstood death with dignity, grace, and forgiveness.

We need never tremble in fear before God. God can be trusted. But trust in God does include a healthy fear because one particular fear, properly understood, is part of the anatomy of love itself. The scriptures say that the fear of the Lord is the beginning of wisdom. But that fear, a healthy fear, must be understood as a reverence, a loving awe, a love that fears disappointing. Healthy fear is love's fear, a fear of betraying, of not being faithful to what love asks of us in return for its gratuity. We aren't afraid of someone we trust, fearing that he or she will suddenly turn arbitrary, unfair, cruel, incomprehensible, vicious, unloving. Rather, we are afraid about how worthy we are of the trust that's given to us, not least from God.

But we must trust that God understands our humanity: God doesn't demand that we give him our conscious attention all of the time. God accepts the natural wanderings of our hearts. God accepts our tiredness and fatigue. God accepts our need for distraction and escape. God accepts that we usually find it easier to immerse ourselves in entertainment than to pray. And God even accepts our resistance to him and our need to assert, with pride, our own independence. Like a loving mother embracing a child who's kicking and screaming but needs to be picked up and held, God can handle our anger, self-pity, and resistance. God understands our humanity, but we struggle to understand what it means to be human before God.

For many years, I feared that I was too immersed in the things of this world to consider myself a spiritual person, always fearing that God wanted more from me. I felt that I should be spending more time in prayer, but too often I'd end up too tired to pray, more interested in watching a sports event on television or sitting around with family, colleagues, or friends, talking about everything except spiritual things. For years, I feared that God wanted me to be more explicitly spiritual. He probably did! But, as I've aged, I've come to realize that being with God in prayer and being with God in heart is like being with a trusted friend. In an easeful friendship, friends don't spend most of their time talking about their mutual friendship. They talk about everything else instead: local gossip, the weather, their work, their children, their headaches, their heartaches, their tiredness, what they saw on television the night before, their favorite sports teams, what's happening in politics, and the jokes they've heard recently—though they occasionally lament that they should ideally be talking more about deeper things. Should they?

John of the Cross teaches that in any long-term friendship the important things eventually begin to happen under the surface. Think of casual conversation as the tip of an iceberg. The real power is moving along underneath the waters. Togetherness, ease with each other, comfort, and the sense of being at home are what we give each other then.

That's also true for our relationship with God. God made us to be human, and God wants us, with all of our wandering weaknesses, to be human in his presence, with ease, with comfort, and with the feeling that we are at home. Our fear of God can be reverence or timidity; the former is healthy, the latter is neurotic.

Holy and Unholy Fear of God

Not all fear is created equal, at least not religiously. There's a fear that's healthy and good, a sign of maturity and love. There's also a fear that's bad, that blocks maturity and love. It can be difficult at times to know the difference.

There's a lot of misunderstanding about fear inside religious circles, especially around the scriptural passage that says that the fear of God is the beginning of wisdom. Too often texts like these, as well as religion in general, have been used to instill in people an unhealthy fear in the name of God. We need to live in "holy fear," but holy fear is a very particular kind of fear that should not be confused with fear as we normally understand it.

What is "holy fear"? What kind of fear is healthy? What kind of fear triggers wisdom?

Holy fear is love's fear—namely, the kind of fear that is inspired by love. It's a fear based upon reverence and respect for a person or a thing we love. When we genuinely love another person we will live inside a healthy anxiety, a worry that our actions should never grossly disappoint, disrespect, or violate the other person. We live in holy fear when we are anxious not to betray a trust or disrespect someone. But this is very different from being afraid of somebody or being afraid of being punished.

Bad power and bad authority intimidate and make others afraid of them. God is never that kind of power or authority. God entered our world as a helpless infant, and God's power still takes that same modality. Babies don't intimidate, even as they inspire holy fear. We watch our words and our actions around babies not because they threaten us, but because their very helplessness and innocence inspire an anxiety in us that makes us want to be at our best around them.

The Gospels are meant to inspire that kind of fear. God is Love, a benevolent power, a gracious authority, not someone to be feared. Indeed, God is the last person we need to fear. Jesus came to rid us of fear. Virtually every theophany in the scriptures (an instance where God appears) begins with the words: "Do not be afraid!" What frightens us does not come from God.

In the Hebrew Bible, King David is revealed as the person who best grasped this. Among all the figures in the Old Testament, including Moses and the great prophets, David is depicted as the figure who best exemplifies what it means to walk on this earth in the image and likeness of God, even though at a point he grossly abuses that trust. Despite his great sin, it is David, not Moses or the prophets, to whom Jesus attributes his lineage. David is the Christ figure in the Old Testament. He walked in holy fear of God, and never in an unhealthy fear.

To cite just one salient example: The first book of Samuel recounts an incident where David is returning from battle with his soldiers one day. His troops are hungry. The only available food is the bread in the temple. David asks for that and is told that it is only to be consumed by the priests in sacred ritual. He answers the priest to this effect: "I'm the king, placed here by God to act responsibly in his name. We don't ordinarily ask for the temple bread, but this is an exception, a matter of urgency, the soldiers need food, and God would want us to responsibly do this." And so he took the temple bread and gave it to his soldiers. In the Gospels, Jesus praises this action by David and asks us to imitate it, telling us that we are not made for the Sabbath but that the Sabbath is made for us.

David understood what is meant by that. He had discerned that God is not so much a law to be obeyed as a gracious presence under which we are asked to creatively live. He feared God, but as one fears someone in love, with a "holy fear," not a blind, legalistic one.

A young mother once shared this story with me: Her six-year-old had just started school. She had taught him to kneel by his bed each night before going to sleep and recite a number of prayers. One night, shortly after starting school, he hopped into bed without first kneeling in prayer. Surprised by this, she challenged him: "Don't you pray anymore?" His reply: "No, I don't. My teacher at school told us that we are not supposed to pray. She said that we're supposed to talk to God . . . and tonight I'm tired and have nothing to say!"

Like King David, he too had discerned what it really means to be God's child and how God is not so much a law to be obeyed as a gracious presence who desires a mutually loving relationship, one of holy fear.

Fear of Hell

Hell is never a nasty surprise waiting for a basically happy person. Hell can only be the full flowering of a pride and selfishness that have, through a long time, twisted a heart so thoroughly that it considers happiness as unhappiness and has an arrogant disdain for happy people. If you are essentially warm of heart this side of eternity, you need not fear that a nasty surprise awaits you on the other side because somewhere along the line, unknowingly, you missed the boat and your life went terribly wrong.

Unfortunately for many of us who came of age in the middle of the twentieth century, we were taught something very different. You could live your life sincerely, in essential honesty, relate fairly to others, try your best given your weaknesses, have some bounce and happiness in life, and then die and find that some sin you'd committed or mistake you'd made, perhaps even unknowingly, could doom you to hell, and there was no further chance for repentance. The second before your death was your last chance to change things, no do-overs after death, no matter how badly you might like then to repent. As a tree falls so shall it lie! We were schooled to fear dying and the afterlife.

But, whatever the practical effectiveness of such a concept, because the fear of hell really could make one hesitate in the face of temptation, it is essentially wrong and should not be taught in the name of Christianity. Why? Because it belies the God and the deep truths that Jesus revealed. Jesus did teach that there was a hell and that it was a possibility for everyone. But the hell that Jesus spoke of is not a place or a state where someone is begging for one last chance, just one more minute of life to make an Act of Contrition, and God is refusing. The God whom Jesus both incarnates and reveals is a God who is forever open to repentance, forever open to contrition, and forever waiting for our return from our prodigal wanderings.

With God we never exhaust our chances. Can you imagine God looking at a repentant man or woman and saying, "Sorry! For you, it's too late! You had your chance! Don't come asking for another chance now!" That could not be the Father of Jesus.

And yet the Gospels at times can give us that impression. We have, for example, the famous parable of the rich man who ignores the poor man at his doorstep, dies, and ends up in hell, while the poor man, Lazarus, whom he had ignored, is now in heaven, comforted in the bosom of Abraham. From his torment in hell, the rich man asks Abraham to send Lazarus to him with some water, but Abraham replies that there is an unbridgeable gap between heaven and hell and no one can cross from one side to the other. That text, along with Jesus's warnings that the doors of the wedding banquet will at a point be irrevocably closed, has led to the common misconception that there is a point of no return, that once in hell, it is too late to repent.

But that's not what this text, nor Jesus's warning on the urgency of repentance, teaches. The "unbridgeable gap" here refers, among other things, to a gap that remains forever unbridged here in this world between the rich and the poor. And it remains unbridged because of our intransigence, our failure to change heart, our lack of contrition, not because God runs out of patience and says, "Enough! No more chances!" It remains unbridged because, habitually, we become so set in our ways that we are incapable of change and genuine repentance.

Jesus's story of the rich man and Lazarus actually draws upon a more ancient Jewish story that illustrates this intransigence: In the parallel Jewish parable, God does hear the rich man's plea from hell for a second chance and grants it to him. The rich man, now full of new resolutions, returns to life, goes immediately to the market, loads his cart with food, and, as he is driving home, meets Lazarus on the road. Lazarus asks for a loaf of bread. The rich man jumps off his cart to give it to him, but as he pulls a huge loaf of bread from his cart, his old self starts to reassert itself. He begins to think, "This man doesn't need a whole loaf! Why not just give him a part! And why should he have a fresh loaf; I'll give him some of the stale bread!" Immediately he finds himself back in hell! He still cannot bridge the gap.

Kathleen Dowling Singh, in the remarkable book *The Grace in Dying*, submits that in making a series of mental contractions we create our own fear of death. That's true too for the afterlife: by making a series of unfortunate theological contractions we create our own fear of hell.

Trust in God as the Antidote to Fear

A number of years ago, I was at the funeral of a young man who had died tragically in a car accident. At the time of his death, on the surface, his relationship to his church and to some of its moral teachings was far from ideal: he was not attending church regularly, was living with his girlfriend outside marriage, was not much concerned about the poor or the larger community, and was, in simple terms, partying pretty hard. But everyone who knew him also knew of his essential goodness and his wonderful heart. There wasn't an ounce of malice in him, and heaven would be forever a less colorful and more impoverished place if he weren't there. At the reception following the church service, one of his aunts said to me, "He was such a good person, if I were running the gates of heaven, I would certainly let him in." I assured her that no doubt God felt the same way, given that God's understanding and forgiveness infinitely surpass our own.

We harbor too many unconscious fears of God: Fear that God is not as understanding and compassionate as we are. Fear that God is not as bighearted as we are (or fear that God may be as small-hearted as we are). Fear that God does not read the heart and cannot tell the difference between wound and coldness, immaturity and sin. Fear that God gives us only one chance and cannot bear any missteps and infidelities. Fear that God doesn't respect our humanity, that God created us in one way but wants us to live in another way in order to be saved. Fear that God is threatened by our achievements, like a petty tyrant. Fear that God is threatened by our doubts and questions, like an insecure leader. Fear that God cannot stand up to the intellectual and cultural scrutiny of our world but somehow needs to be segregated and protected like an overpious novice. Fear that God is less interested in our lives than we are and less solicitous for our salvation and that of our loved ones than we are. And, not least, fear that God is as helpless before our moral helplessness as we are.

But that is not the God we believe in.

CHAPTER FOUR

Wrestling with the Gospel Mandate to Reach Out to the Poor

*Nobody gets to heaven without
a letter of reference from the poor.*

—JAMES FORBES

Being Good-Hearted Is Not Enough

Charity is about being good-hearted, but justice is about something more. Individual sympathy is good and virtuous, but it doesn't necessarily change the social, economic, and political structures that unfairly victimize some people and unduly privilege others. We need to be fair and good of heart, but we also need to have fair and good policies.

Jim Wallis, the founder of *Sojourners*, speaking more specifically about racism, puts it this way: When we protest that we are not implicated in unjust systems by saying things like "I have black friends," we need to challenge ourselves. It's not just what's in our hearts that's at issue; it's also what's at the heart of public policy. We can have black friends, but if our policies are racist there's still no justice in the land. Individual goodwill alone doesn't always make for a system that's fair to everyone.

And it's precisely on this point where we see the crucial distinction between charity and justice, between being good-hearted as individuals and trying as a community to ensure that our social, economic, and political systems are not themselves the cause of the very things we are trying to respond to in charity. What causes poverty, racism, economic disparity, lack of fair access to education and health care, and the irresponsibility with which we often treat nature? Individual attitudes, true. But injustice is also the result of social, economic, and political policies that, whatever their other merits, help produce the conditions that spawn poverty, inequality, racism, privilege, and the lack of conscientious concern for the air we breathe.

Most of us, I suspect, are familiar with a story that's often used to distinguish between charity and justice. It runs this way: There was a town built alongside a river, but situated around a bend so that the townsfolk could see only that part of the river that bordered their town. One day a few of the children were playing by the river when they saw five bodies floating in the water. They quickly ran for help and the townspeople they alerted did what any responsible persons would do in that situation. They took care of the bodies. Pulling them from the river they found that two were dead and they buried them. Three were still alive. One was a child for whom they quickly found a foster home; another was a severely ill woman whom they put in a hospital; the last was a young man, and they found him a job and a place to live.

But the story didn't end there. The next day more bodies appeared and, again, the townsfolk responded as before. They took care of the bodies. They buried the dead, placed the sick in hospitals, and found foster homes for the children, and jobs and places to live for the adults. And so it went on for years; taking care of the bodies they found each day became a normal feature of their lives and part of the life of their churches and their community. A few altruistically motivated people even made it their life's work to take care of those bodies.

But—and this is the point—nobody ever went up the river to see from where and for what reasons those bodies kept appearing downstream each day. They just remained good-hearted and generous in their response to the bodies that found their way to their town.

The lesson is clear enough: It's one thing (needed, good, and Christian) to take care of the needy bodies we find on our doorsteps, but it's another thing (also needed, good, and Christian) to go upstream to try to change the things that are causing those bodies to be in the river. That's the difference between good-hearted charity and acting for social justice.

Sadly, though, as good churchgoing Christians we have been too slow to grasp this and consequently have not brought the demands of Jesus and faith to bear as strongly upon the question of social justice as we have been to bring them to bear upon charity. Too many good, good-hearted, churchgoing, charitable women and men simply do not see the demands of justice as being anything beyond the demands of private charity and good-heartedness. And so we are often good-hearted enough that we will, literally, give a needy person the shirt off our back even as we refuse to look at why our closets are overflowing while some others don't have a shirt.

But this should not be misunderstood. The Gospel demand that we act for justice does not in any way denigrate the virtue of charity. Charity is still the ultimate virtue, and sometimes the only positive difference we can make in our world is precisely the one-to-one love and respect that we give to each other. Our own individual goodness is sometimes the only candle that is ours to light.

But that goodness and light must shine publicly too—namely, in how we vote and in what public policies we support or oppose.

Our Innate Need to Be Generous

We need to give to the poor not because they need it, though they do, but because we need to do that in order to be healthy. That's an axiom that is grounded in the scriptures where, time and again, we are taught that giving to the poor is something that we need to do for our own health.

We see this truth expressed in many religions and cultures. For example, indigenous North American peoples practice something they call potlatch. This is a festival, sometimes attached to the celebration of a birth or a wedding, at which a rich person gives gifts to the community. Its primary purpose is to ensure not only a certain distribution of wealth but also the health of wealthy individuals in terms of not accumulating too much wealth. Too much excess, it is believed, leaves a person unhealthy. This has been a perennial belief in most cultures.

In Christianity we have enshrined this truth in the challenge to be charitable to the poor, and we have classically seen our giving to the poor as a virtue, and rightly so. Charitable giving is a virtue; but, for a Christian, perhaps it's more obligation than virtue. When we look at the Law of Moses in the scriptures we see that a certain amount of giving to the poor was prescribed by law. The idea was that giving to the poor was an obligation, not a negotiable moral option. Simply put, the Law of Moses legally obligated people to give to the poor.

The scriptures abound with examples; consider these precepts and laws:

First of all, the Law of Moses assumed that everything we have belongs to God and is not really ours. We are only its stewards and guardians. We may enjoy it at God's pleasure, but ultimately it's not ours (Leviticus 25:23).

Every seventh year, all slaves were to be set free and each was to take with him or her enough of the master's goods to be able to live an independent life (Deuteronomy 15:14).

Every seventh year all economic debts were to be canceled (the original meaning of the "statute of limitations").

Every seventh year one's land was to lie fallow and enjoy its own Sabbath. During that year, the land's owner not only didn't sow anything; he or she didn't reap anything either. The poor were to reap whatever the fields and vineyards produced that year.

And, at all times, landowners were forbidden to reap and harvest the corners of their fields, with the intent that these edges were to be reaped by the poor.

Finally, even more radically, every fiftieth year all lands were to be restored to the original tribe or household who had first owned them. One's "ownership" of property had a certain time limit. Things weren't yours forever.

Moreover, doing all of this was a legal obligation, not an optional virtuous deed.

We have much to learn from this as a society. For the

most part, we are generous and charitable people. We give away some of our surplus, and despite warnings from professionals who work with street people that this isn't helpful, our hearts are still moved by those begging on our streets and we continue to slip them money (even as we don't believe their claims that they need money for food or bus fare). For the most part, our hearts are still in the right place.

But we tend to see this as something we are doing purely for someone else without realizing that our own health is a vital part of the equation. Further, we tend to see this as virtue more than obligation, as charity more than justice. And perhaps it's for this reason that, despite our good hearts and our generosity, the gap between the rich and the poor, both within our own culture and within the world as a whole, continues to widen. Millions and millions of people are falling through the cracks without getting the benefit, in law, to reap the corners of our wealth and have their debts forgiven every seven years.

We need to give to the poor because they need it, admittedly; but we need to do it too because we cannot be healthy unless we do this. And we need to see our giving not so much as charity but as obligation, as justice, as something we owe.

On his deathbed, Vincent de Paul is reputed to have challenged his followers with words to this effect: it is more blessed to give than to receive—and it is also easier!

Jesus as Expanding the Concept of Giving

As we have just seen from the Jewish scriptures, we need to give away some of our own possessions in order to be healthy. Wealth that is hoarded always corrupts those who possess it. Any gift that is not shared turns sour. If we are not generous with our gifts, we will be bitterly envied and will eventually turn bitter ourselves. Those truths are written inside human experience and inside every authentic ethical and faith tradition. Hindu, Buddhist, and Islamic spiritualities, each in its own way, affirms this: it is only in giving away some of our gifts that we ourselves can remain healthy.

In Jewish spirituality, blessing is always intended to flow through the person receiving it so as to enrich others. As well, the great Jewish prophets taught that God has a preferential love for the poor. Jesus takes this further. In Chapter 25 of Matthew's Gospel, he teaches that not only does God have a preferential love for the poor, but also God is in the poor! Whatsoever you do to the poor, you are doing to God. How we treat the poor is how we are treating God, and ignorance of that will be no excuse when we come to judgment. Nobody will get to heaven without a letter of reference from the poor. When we stand before God and are judged, Jesus tells us, there will be only one set of criteria—namely, how we gave to the poor: Did you feed the hungry? Give drink to the thirsty? Clothe the naked?

And Jesus has other strong teachings about how we handle being rich and how we treat the poor: For instance, the Gospel of Luke, a Gospel within which Jesus warns us that it is easier for a camel to pass through the eye of a needle than for a rich person to enter the kingdom of heaven, he nevertheless praises the rich who are generous, condemning only the rich who are stingy. For Luke, generosity is the key to health and heaven. Finally, even more strongly, in the story of the widow who gives her last two pennies away, Luke 21:1–4, Jesus challenges us not only to give of our surplus to the poor but also to give away some of what we need to live on. The Gospels, and the rest of the Christian scriptures, strongly challenge us to give to the poor—not because they need our charity, though they do, but because our giving to them is the only way we can stay healthy.

A Message Taken Up by the Churches

The Christian churches have taken up this message from Jesus and have always challenged Christians to be both charitable and just to the poor. Of course, the historical record of the churches on this has not always been stellar, particularly in regard to social justice. We have been, and remain, stronger on private charity than on social justice, in that many Christians will give food or clothing to a needy person but, at the same time, refuse to look at what within our way of life creates poverty and needy people.

As well, too often, both in our preaching and in our very ethos, we have mistaken the gospel of prosperity for the Gospel of Jesus.

Irrespective of our weaknesses and inconsistencies on this, the churches have throughout the centuries formulated a clear and strong social doctrine. Sadly, too few Christians are aware of Christian social doctrine and believe that private charity alone is all that is asked for by our Christian faith. Christian social doctrine is, as is sometimes quipped, the best-kept secret in the world.

What is Christian social doctrine? Let me here, for critics and faithful alike, list, in caption form, some of the main tenets of that long tradition. With little difference among the various churches, Christian spirituality teaches, and has taught for a long time, these moral truths:

1. All people in the world have equal dignity and should enjoy equal rights in terms of respect, access to resources, and access to opportunity.

2. God intended the earth for all persons equally. Thus the riches of this world should flow equally and fairly to all. All other rights, including the right to private property and the accumulation of riches that are fairly earned, must be subordinated to this more primary principle.

3. The right to private property and accumulation of wealth is not an absolute one. It must be subordinated to the common good, to the fact that the goods of the earth are intended equally for all. No one has the moral right to keep as much as he or she can earn without concern for the common good (even if he or she is a celebrity).

4. No person, group of persons, or nation may have a surplus of goods if others lack the basic necessities.

5. We are obliged, morally, to come to the aid of those in need. In giving such aid, we are not doing charity, but serving justice. Helping the poor is not an issue of personal virtue and generosity, but something that is demanded by justice itself.

6. The laws of supply and demand, free enterprise, unbridled competition, the profit motive, and private ownership of the means of production may not be seen as morally inviolate and must, when the common good or justice demand, be balanced off by other principles.

7. Physical nature too has inherent rights—namely, rights that are intrinsic to itself

and not simply given to it because of its relationship to humanity. The earth is not just a stage for human beings to play on, but is a creature of God with its own rights that humans may not violate.

8. The present situation within the world, where some individuals and nations have excess while others lack the basic necessities, is immoral, goes against the teachings of Christ, and must be redressed.

9. The condemnation of injustice is part of the church's essential ministry of preaching and is an essential aspect of the church's prophetic role.

10. Movement toward the poor is a privileged route toward both God and spiritual health. There can be no spiritual health, individually and communally, when there is no real involvement with the struggles of the poor. Conversely, riches of all kinds are dangerous.

A Special Challenge in a Time of Refugees and Globalization

In the Hebrew scriptures, we find a strong religious challenge to always welcome the stranger, the foreigner. This was emphasized for two reasons: First, the Jewish people themselves had once been foreigners and immigrants. Their scriptures kept reminding them not to forget that. Second, they believed that God's revelation most often comes to us through the stranger, in what's foreign to us. That belief was integral to their faith.

The great prophets developed this much further. They taught that God favors the poor preferentially and that consequently we will be judged—judged religiously—by how we treat the poor. The prophets coined this verse (still worth memorizing): "The quality of your faith will be judged by the quality of justice in the land; and the quality of justice in the land will always be judged by how orphans, widows, and strangers fare while you are alive."

Orphans, widows, and strangers! That's scriptural code for who, at any given time, are the three most vulnerable groups in society. And the prophets' message didn't go down easy. Rather, it was a religious affront to many of the pious at the time who strongly believed that we will be judged religiously and morally by the rigor and strictness of our religious observance. Then, like now, social justice was often religiously marginalized.

But Jesus sides with the Hebrew prophets. For him, God not only makes a preferential option for the poor, but, as noted earlier, God is in the poor. How we treat the poor is how we treat God. Moreover, the prophets' maxim that we will be judged religiously by how we treat the poor is given a normative expression in Jesus's discourse on the final judgment in Chapter 25 of the Gospel of Matthew. We are all familiar, perhaps too familiar, with that text. Jesus, in effect, was answering a series of questions: What will the last judgment be like? What will be the test? How will we be judged?

His answer is stunning and, taken baldly, is perhaps the most challenging text in the Gospels. He tells us that we will be judged, seemingly solely, on the basis of how we treated the poor—that is, on how we have treated the most vulnerable among us. At one point, he even singles out "the stranger," the foreigner, the refugee: "I was a stranger and you made me welcome . . . or . . . you never made me welcome." We end up on the right or wrong side of God on the basis of how we treat the stranger.

What also needs to be highlighted in this text about the last judgment is that neither those who got it right nor those who got it wrong knew what they were doing. Both groups initially protest: the former by saying, "We didn't know it was you we were serving," and the latter by saying, "Had we known it was you we would have responded." Both protests, it would seem, are beside the point. In Matthew's Gospel, mature discipleship doesn't depend upon our believing that we have it right, it depends only upon our doing it right.

These scriptural principles, I believe, are very apropos today in the face of the refugee and immigrant issues we are contending with in the Western world. Today, without doubt, we are facing the biggest humanitarian crisis since the end of the Second World War. Millions upon millions of people, under unjust persecution and the threat of death, are being driven from their homes and homelands with no place to go and no country or community willing to receive them. As Christians we may not turn our backs on them or turn them away. If Jesus is to be believed, we will be judged religiously more by how we treat refugees than by whether or not we are going to church. When we stand before God in judgment and say in protest, "When did I see you a stranger and not welcome you?" our generation is likely to hear, "I was a Syrian refugee, and you did not welcome me."

Undoubtedly, this might sound naive, overidealistic, and fundamentalist. The issue of refugees and immigrants is both highly sensitive and very complex. Countries have borders that need to be respected and defended, just as their citizens have a right to be protected. Admittedly, there are very real political, social, economic, and security issues that have to be addressed. But as we, our churches, and our governments address them, we must remain clear on what the scriptures, Jesus, and the social teachings of the church uncompromisingly teach: we are to welcome the stranger, irrespective of inconvenience and even if there are some dangers.

For all sorts of pragmatic reasons—political, social,

economic, and security—we can perhaps justify not welcoming the stranger, but we can never justify this on Christian grounds. Not welcoming a stranger is antithetical to the very heart of Jesus's message and makes us too easily forget that we too were once the outsider.

A Healthy Attitude Toward Wealth

The rich are getting richer, and we are almost beyond surprise at how rich that is.

Every day, the newspapers, the cable networks, and the Internet report financial compensations that were unimaginable just a generation ago: corporate executives receiving hundred-million-dollar bonuses, athletes and entertainers signing contracts for tens of millions, people in information technology earning billions, and ordinary folks everywhere joining the millionaire club.

And what's our reaction? It's difficult to judge. We express indignation and protest that this wealth explosion is out of proportion, even as we nurse a not-so-secret envy: I wish it were me!

As a society we adore the rich and famous, pure and simple, and in the end, despite our envy, we grant them their due: Good for them! They worked for it. They have the talent. They deserve all they get!

But how should we view being rich from a faith perspective? Jesus warned that riches are dangerous both to the soul and to society. How should this warning affect our attitude toward our own wealth and that of others?

First, we must never idealize poverty and see wealth as a bad thing in itself. God is rich, not poor, and heaven will not be a place of poverty. Poverty is something to overcome and eradicate. The poor don't enjoy being poor. Next, we must not be too quick to politicize both poverty and wealth. Our lens must always be moral rather than political, though obviously both wealth and poverty have huge political implications. Finally, before we attack wealth and those who possess it, we must ensure that we are free from embittered moralizing, which is little more than envy.

What principles should guide us in terms of an attitude toward wealth?

Underlying everything else, we must always keep in mind Jesus's warning that the possession of wealth is dangerous, that it is hard for a rich person to enter the kingdom of heaven. This warning will help us to accept two principles:

First, the possession of wealth is not a bad thing in and of itself; what can be bad is how we use it and what it can do to our hearts. Jesus makes a distinction between the generous rich and the miserly rich. The former are good because they imitate God; the latter are bad. When we are generous, particularly in a very prodigious way, riches won't close our hearts. But the reverse is also true. All miserliness, all stinginess, all lack of generosity closes our hearts in ways that make it hard to enter the kingdom of heaven or genuine human community, to put it in purely human terms. The generous rich can inherit the kingdom; the miserly rich cannot.

Second, what we have is not our own; it's given to us in trust. God is the sole owner of all that is, and the world properly belongs to everyone. We need to remember that it wasn't just our own ingenuity and hard work that gave us what we view as our own. The fruits of our labor are also the fruits of other people's labor. We too easily lose sight of that. Here's how Bill Gates Sr. put it in the January–February 2003 issue of *Sojourners*:

> Society has an enormous claim upon the fortunes of the wealthy. This is rooted not only in most religious traditions, but also in an honest accounting of society's substantial investment in creating fertile ground for wealth-creation. Judaism, Christianity, and Islam all affirm the right of individual ownership and private property, but there are moral limits imposed on absolute private ownership of wealth and property. Each tradition affirms that we are not individuals alone but exist in community—a community that makes claims on us. The notion that "it is all mine" is a violation of these

teachings and traditions. Society's claim on individual accumulated wealth is . . . rooted in the recognition of society's direct and indirect investment in the individual's success. In other words, we didn't get there on our own.

✥

CHAPTER FIVE

Wrestling with Faith and Doubt

*Learn to understand more by
not understanding than by understanding.*

—JOHN OF THE CROSS

The Hiddenness of God

When I first began teaching theology, I fantasized about writing a book about the hiddenness of God. Why does God remain hidden and invisible? Why doesn't God just show himself plainly in a way that nobody can dispute?

One of the standard answers to those questions was this: If God did manifest himself plainly there wouldn't be any need for faith. But that left us with new questions: Who wants faith? Wouldn't it be better to just plainly see God? There were other answers to those questions, of course, except I didn't know them or didn't grasp them with enough depth for them to be meaningful. For example, one such answer taught that God is pure Spirit and cannot be perceived through our normal human senses. But that seemed too abstract to me. And so I began to search for different answers or for better articulations of our stock answers to those questions. And there was a pot of gold at the end of the search; it led me to the mystics, particularly John of the Cross, and to spiritual writers such as Carlo Carretto.

What's their answer? They offer no simple answers. What they offer instead are various perspectives that throw light on the ineffability of God, the mystery of faith, and the mystery of human knowing in general. In essence, how we know as human beings, and how we know God, is deeply paradoxical; that is, the more deeply we know anything, the more that person or object begins to become less conceptually clear. One of the most famous mystics in history suggests that as we enter into deeper intimacy we concomitantly enter into a "cloud of unknowing"—namely, into a knowing so deep that it can no longer be conceptualized. What does this mean?

Three analogies can help us here: *a baby in its mother's womb; darkness as excessive light;* and *deep intimacy as breaking down our conceptual images.*

First: Imagine a baby in its mother's womb. In the womb, the baby is so totally enveloped and surrounded by the mother that, paradoxically, it cannot see the mother and cannot have any concept of the mother. Its inability to see or picture its mother is caused by the mother's omnipresence, not by her absence. The mother is too present, too all enveloping, to be seen or conceptualized. The baby has to be born to see its mother. The same holds true for us in terms of seeing God. The scriptures tell us that we live, and move, and breathe, and have our being in God. We are in God's womb, enveloped by God, and, like a baby, we must first be born (death as our second birth) to see God face-to-face. That is faith's darkness.

Second: Excessive light is darkness. If you stare straight into the sun with an unshielded eye, what do you see? Nothing. The very excess of light renders you as blind as if you were in pitch darkness. And that's also the reason why we have difficulty in seeing God: generally, the deeper we journey into intimacy with God, the deeper we are journeying into the Light, the more God seems to disappear and become harder and harder to picture or imagine. We're being blinded, not by God's absence, but by the blinding light of his presence. The darkness of faith is the darkness of excessive light.

Third: Deep intimacy is iconoclastic. The deeper our intimacy with anyone the more our pictures and images of that person begin to break down. Imagine this: A friend says to you, "I understand you perfectly: I know your family, your background, your ethnicity, your psychological and emotional temperaments, your strengths, your weaknesses, and your habits. I understand you." Would you feel understood? I suspect not. Now imagine a very different scenario: A friend says to you, "You're a mystery to me! I've known you for years, but you have a depth that's somehow beyond me. The longer I know you, the more I know that you are your own mystery." In this nonunderstanding, in being allowed to be the full mystery of your own person in that friend's understanding, you would, paradoxically, feel much better understood. John of the Cross submits that the deeper we journey into intimacy, the more *we will begin to understand by not understanding than by understanding.* Our relationship to God works in the same way. Initially, when our intimacy is not so deep, we feel that we understand things and we have firm feelings and ideas about God. But the deeper we journey, the more those feelings and ideas will begin to feel false and empty because our growing intimacy is opening us to the fuller mystery of God. Paradoxically, this feels like God is disappearing and becoming nonexistent.

Faith, by definition, implies a paradoxical darkness: the closer we get to God in this life, the more God seems to disappear, because overpowering light can seem like darkness.

So Faith Works Quietly

The poet Rumi submits that we live with a deep secret that sometimes we know, and then not.

That can be very helpful in understanding our faith. One of the reasons why we struggle with faith is that God's presence inside us and in our world is rarely dramatic, overwhelming, sensational, something impossible to ignore. God doesn't work like that. Rather, God's presence, much to our frustration and loss of patience sometimes, is something that lies quiet and seemingly helpless inside us. It rarely makes a huge splash.

Because we are not sufficiently aware of this, we tend to misunderstand the dynamics of faith and find ourselves habitually trying to ground our faith on precisely something that is loud and dramatic. We are forever looking for something beyond what God gives us. But we should know from the very way God was born into our world that faith needs to ground itself on something that is quiet and undramatic. Jesus, as we know, was born into our world with no fanfare and no power, a baby lying helpless in the straw, another child among millions. Nothing spectacular to human eyes surrounded his birth. Then, during his ministry, he never performed miracles to prove his divinity, but only as acts of compassion or to reveal something about God. Jesus never used divine power in an attempt to prove that God exists beyond doubt. His ministry, like his birth, wasn't an attempt to prove God's existence. It was intended rather to teach us what God is like and that God loves us unconditionally.

Moreover, Jesus's teaching about God's presence in our lives also makes clear that this presence is mostly quiet and hidden, a plant growing silently as we sleep, yeast leavening dough in a manner hidden from our eyes, summer slowly turning a barren tree green, an insignificant mustard plant eventually surprising us with its growth, a man or woman forgiving an enemy. God, it seems, works in ways that are quiet and hidden from our eyes. The God that Jesus incarnates is neither dramatic nor splashy.

And there's an important faith lesson in this. Simply put, God lies inside us, deep inside, but in a way that's almost nonexistent, almost unfelt, largely unnoticed, and easily ignored. However, while that presence is never overpowering, it has within it a gentle, unremitting imperative, a compulsion toward something higher, which invites us to draw upon it. And, if we do draw upon it, it gushes up in us in an infinite stream that instructs us, nurtures us, and fills us with endless energy.

This is important for understanding faith. God lies inside us as an invitation that fully respects our freedom, never overpowers us, but also never goes away. It lies there precisely like a baby lying helpless in the straw, gently beckoning us, but helpless in itself to make us pick it up.

For example, C. S. Lewis, in explaining why he finally became, in his words, "the most dejected and reluctant convert in all of England," writes that for years he was able to effectively ignore a voice inside him precisely because it was almost nonexistent, almost unfelt, and largely unnoticed. On the other hand, in retrospect, he realized it had always been there, a gentle, incessant nudge, beckoning him to draw from it, something he eventually recognized as a gentle but unyielding imperative, a "compulsion" that, if obeyed, leads to liberation.

Ruth Burrows, the British Carmelite and mystic, describes a similar experience in her autobiography, *Before the Living God*. Chronicling her late adolescent years, Burrows describes both her religious flightiness and her lack of attraction to the religious life. Yet she eventually ends up not only being serious about religion but becoming a Carmelite nun. What happened? One day, in a chapel, almost against her will, triggered by a series of accidental circumstances, she opened herself to a voice inside her that she had, until then, mainly ignored because it lay inside her precisely as a voice that was almost nonexistent, almost unfelt, and largely unnoticed. But once touched, it gushed up as the deepest and most real thing inside her and set the direction of her life forever afterward. Like C. S. Lewis, she too, once she had opened herself to it, felt it as an unyielding moral compulsion opening her to ultimate liberation.

Why doesn't God show himself to us more directly and

more powerfully so as to make faith easier? That's a fair question for which there is no fully satisfying answer. But the answer we do have lies in understanding the manner in which God manifests himself in our lives and in our world. Unlike most everything else that's trying to get our attention, God never tries to overwhelm us. God, more than anyone else, respects our freedom. For this reason, God lies everywhere, inside us and around us, almost unfelt, largely unnoticed, and easily ignored, a quiet, gentle nudge, but, if drawn upon, the ultimate stream of love and energy.

The Dynamics of Faith—Walking on Water and Sinking Like a Stone

Faith isn't something you ever simply achieve. It's not something that you ever nail down as a fait accompli. Faith works this way: some days you walk on water and other days you sink like a stone. Faith invariably gives way to doubt before it again recovers its confidence, then it loses it again.

We see this graphically illustrated in the well-known Gospel story of Peter walking on water. The disciples had just witnessed a major miracle, Jesus feeding more than five thousand people with five loaves of bread and two fish. Having just witnessed a miracle, their faith was strong. Soon afterward they get into a boat to cross a lake. Jesus is not with them. A few miles out they run into a fierce storm and begin to panic. Jesus comes walking toward them on the water. They're frightened at first and take him for a ghost. But he calms their fear by telling them, right from the center of the storm, that he is not just Jesus but that he is God's very presence.

Peter is immediately buoyed up in his faith and asks Jesus to let him too walk on the water. Jesus invites him to do so and Peter gets out of the boat confidently and begins to walk on the water. But then, realizing what he is doing and the incredible nature of it, he immediately starts to sink and cries out for help; Jesus has to reach out and rescue him from drowning.

What we see illustrated here are two things that lie at the heart of our experience of faith: (1) faith (literally) has its ups and downs and (2) faith works best when we don't confuse it with our own powers.

The incident of Peter walking on the water illustrates that faith has its ups and downs. As he confidently steps onto the sea and begins to walk, his faith feels strong. But almost immediately upon realizing what he is doing, he starts to sink. Our own faith works exactly like that: sometimes it lets us walk on water and sometimes we sink like a stone. The Gospel image of Peter walking on the sea and then splashing in speaks for itself.

However, if we feel discouraged because our faith vacillates in this way, we can take consolation from these words by the English mystic Julian of Norwich. Describing one of her visions, she writes:

After this He [Jesus] showed a most excellent spiritual pleasure in my soul: I was completely filled with everlasting certainty, powerfully sustained without any painful fear. This feeling was so joyful and so spiritual that I was wholly in peace and in repose and there was nothing on earth that would have grieved me. This lasted only a while, and I was changed and left to myself in such sadness and weariness of my life, and annoyance with myself that scarcely was I able to have patience to live. . . . And immediately after this, our Blessed Lord gave me again the comfort and the rest in my soul, in delight and in security so blissful and so powerful that no fear, no sorrow, no bodily pain that could be suffered would have distressed me. And then pain showed again to my feeling, and then the joy and delight, and now the one, and now the other, various times.

Julian of Norwich was a renowned mystic with an exceptional faith and yet, like Peter, she too vacillated between walking on water and sinking like a stone. Her confident feelings came—but they also left.

In the same vein, faith works best when we don't confuse it with our own efforts. For example, the late British spiritual writer Donald Nicholl, in his book *Holiness*, shares the story of a British missionary working in Africa who was called upon to mediate a dispute between two tribes early on in his stay there. Naive and totally out of his depth, he had no preparation for such negotiations. But he gave himself over to the task in faith and, surprisingly, reconciled the two tribes. Afterward, buoyed by this success, he began to fancy himself as a mediator and presented himself as an arbiter of disputes. But now his efforts were invariably unhelpful. Here's the irony: when he didn't know what he was doing, but trusted solely in God, he was able to walk on water; as soon as he began to wrap himself in the process, he sank like a stone. Faith works like that: we can walk on water only as long as we don't think that we are doing it with our own strength.

Rumi once wrote that we live with a deep secret that sometimes we know, and then not, and then we know it again. Faith works like that: some days we walk on water, other days we sink like a stone, and then later we walk on water again.

Faith, Doubt, and Dark Nights of the Soul

Thomas Keating, the renowned spiritual guide, shares with us a line that he occasionally uses in spiritual direction.

People who come to him share how they used to have a warm and solid sense of God in their lives, but now they complain that all that warmth and confidence have disappeared, and they're left struggling with belief and struggling to pray as they used to. They feel a deep sense of loss and invariably this is their question: "What's wrong with me?" Keating's answer: *God is wrong with you!*

In essence this is what Keating is saying: Despite your pain, there is something very right with you. You have moved past being a religious neophyte, past an initiatory stage of religious growth, which was right for you in its time, and are now being led into a deeper, not lesser, faith. Moreover, that loss of fervor has brought you to a fuller maturity. So, in effect, what you're asking is this: I used to be quite sure of myself religiously and, no doubt, probably somewhat arrogant and judgmental. I felt I understood God and religion and I looked with some disdain at the world. Then the bottom fell out of my faith and my certainty and I'm now finding myself a lot less sure of myself, considerably more humble, more empathetic, and less judgmental. What's wrong with me?

Asked in this way, the question answers itself. Clearly that person is growing, not regressing.

"Lost is a place, too!" Christina Crawford wrote those words in her book *Survivor,* describing her own painful journey through darkness into a deeper maturity. To be saved, we have to first realize that we're lost, and usually our lives have to fall apart before we can come to that realization. Sometimes there's no other cure for arrogance and presumption than a painful loss of certitude about our own ideas about God, faith, and religion.

A curious, paradoxical dynamic lies behind this: We tend to confuse faith with our capacity on any given day to conjure up a concept of God and imagine God's existence. Moreover, we think our faith is strongest at those times when we have affective and emotive feelings attached to our imaginings about God. Our faith feels strongest when bolstered by and inflamed by feelings of fervor. Great spiritual writers will tell us that this stage of fervor is a good stage in our faith, but an initiatory one, more commonly experienced when we are neophytes. Experience tends to support this. In the earlier stages of a religious journey it is common to possess strong affective images of and feelings about God. Our relationship with God parallels the relationship between a couple on their honeymoon. On your honeymoon you have strong emotions and possess a particular certainty about your love, but it's a place you come home from. A honeymoon is an initiatory stage in love, a valuable gift, but something that disappears after it has done its work. A honeymoon is not a marriage, though it's often confused with one. It's the same with faith: strong imaginative images of God are not faith, though they're often confused with it.

Strong imaginative images and strong feelings about

God are, in the end, just that—wonderful images, icons. An image is not the reality. An icon can be beautiful and helpful and point us in the right direction, but when mistaken for the reality it becomes an idol. For this reason, the great spiritual writers tell us that at certain moments of our spiritual journey God "takes away" our certainty and deprives us of all the warm feelings in faith. God does this precisely so that we cannot turn our icons into idols, so that we cannot let the experience of faith get in the way of the end of faith itself—namely, an encounter with the reality and person of God.

Mystics such as John of the Cross call this experience of seemingly losing our faith "a dark night of the soul": we used to feel God's presence with a certain warmth and solidity, but now we feel like God is nonexistent and we are left in doubt. This is what Jesus experienced on the cross and this is what Mother Teresa wrote about in her journals.

And while that darkness can be confusing, it can also be maturing: it can help move us from being arrogant, judgmental, religious neophytes to being humble, empathic men and women, living inside a cloud of unknowing, understanding more by not understanding than by understanding, helpfully lost in a darkness we cannot manipulate or control, so as to finally be pushed into genuine faith, hope, and charity.

A Classic Example of a Dark Night of the Soul and What It Means

In *Mother Teresa: Come Be My Light,* a huge volume of her intimate correspondence is made public, and in it we witness what looks like a very intense fifty-year struggle with faith and belief.

Again and again, she describes her religious experience as "dry," "empty," "lonely," "torturous," "dark," "devoid of all feeling." During the last half century of her life, it seems, she was unable to feel or imagine God's existence.

This struggle confused and upset many people. How could this woman, a paradigm of faith, have experienced such doubts?

Some made a judgment that her faith wasn't real. Their view is that she lived the life of a saint but died the death of an atheist. For doctrinaire atheists, her confession of doubt is manna from the abyss. "She was no more exempt from the realization that religion is a human fabrication than any other person, and that her attempted cure was more and more professions of faith could only have deepened the pit that she dug for herself," Christopher Hitchens wrote.

Was Mother Teresa an atheist?

Hardly! In a deeper understanding of faith, her doubts and feelings of abandonment are not only explicable, they're predictable.

Mother Teresa underwent a dark night of the soul. This is what Jesus suffered on the cross when he cried out, "My God, my God, why have you forsaken me?" When he uttered those words, he meant them. At that moment, he felt exactly what Mother Teresa felt so acutely for more than fifty years—namely, the sense that God is absent, that God is dead, that there isn't any God. But this isn't the absence of faith or the absence of God; rather, it is a deeper presence of God, a presence that, precisely because it goes beyond feeling and imagination, can only be felt as an emptiness, a nothingness, an absence, a nonexistence.

But how does this make sense? How can faith feel like doubt? How can God's deeper presence feel like God's nonexistence? And, perhaps most important: Why would faith work like this?

The literature around the dark night of the soul makes this point: Sometimes when we are unable to induce any kind of feeling that God exists, when we are unable to imagine God's existence, the reason is that God is now coming into our lives in such a way that we cannot manipulate the experience through ego, narcissism, self-advantage, self-glorification, and self-mirroring. This purifies our experience of God because only when all of our own lights are off can we grasp divine light in its purity. Only when we are completely empty of ourselves inside an experience, when our heads and hearts are pumping dry, can God touch us in a way that makes it impossible for us to inject ourselves into the experience, so that we are worshipping God, not ourselves.

And this is painful. It is experienced precisely as darkness, emptiness, doubt, abandonment. But this is, in fact, "the test" that we pray God to spare us from whenever we pray Matthew's version of the Lord's Prayer—"Do not put us to the test."

Moreover, this experience is usually given to those who have the maturity to handle it, spiritual athletes, those who pray for and truly want a searing "purity of heart," people like Mother Teresa. They ask Jesus to experience and feel everything as he did. He just answers their prayers!

Henri Nouwen, in a book called *In Memoriam*, shares a similar insight about his mother. She was, he states, the most faith-filled and generous woman he had ever met. So when he stood at her bedside as she was dying he had every right to expect that her death would be a serene witness to a life of deep faith. But what happened, on the surface at least, seemed the exact reverse: she struggled, was seized by doubts, cried out, and died inside a certain darkness. Only later, after prayer and reflection, did this make sense to him. His mother had prayed her whole life to die like Jesus—and so she did! A common soldier dies without fear; Jesus died afraid.

In *The Crucified God*, a remarkable book, Jürgen Moltmann, quoting Hans Joachim Iwand, writes: "Our faith begins at the point where atheists suppose that it must be at an end. Our faith begins with the bleakness and power which is the night of the cross, abandonment, temptation and doubt about everything that exists! Our faith must be born where it is abandoned by all tangible reality; it must be born of nothingness, it must taste this nothingness and be given it to taste in a way that no philosophy of nihilism can imagine."

Mother Teresa understood all of this. That is why her seeming doubt did not lead her away from God and her vocation but instead riveted her to it with a depth and purity that, more than anything else, tell us precisely what faith really is.

Why Do We Experience Dark Nights of the Soul?

Atheism is a parasite that feeds on bad religion. That's why, in the end, atheistic critics are our friends. They hold our feet to the fire.

Friedrich Nietzsche, Ludwig Feuerbach, and Karl Marx, for example, submit that all religious experience is ultimately psychological projection. For them, the God we believe in and who undergirds our churches is, at the end of the day, simply a fantasy we have created for ourselves to serve our own needs. We have created God as opium for comfort and to give ourselves divine permission to do what we want to do.

They're largely correct, but partially wrong, and true

religion takes its root in where they're wrong. Admittedly, they're right in that a lot of religious experience and church life is far from pure, as is evident in our lives. It's hard to deny that we are forever getting our own ambitions and energies mixed up with what we call religious experience. That's why, so often, we—you and I, sincere religious people—don't look like Jesus at all: we're arrogant where we should be humble, judgmental where we should be forgiving, hateful where we should be loving, self-concerned where we should be altruistic, and, not least, spiteful and vicious where we should be understanding and merciful. Our lives and our churches often don't radiate Jesus. Atheism is a needed challenge because far too often we have our own life force confused with God and our own ideologies confused with the Gospels.

Fortunately, God doesn't let us get away with it for long. Rather, as the mystics teach, God inflicts us with a confusing, painful grace called a dark night of the soul. What happens in a dark night of the soul is that we run out of gas religiously: religious experiences that once sustained us and gave us fervor dry up or get crucified in a way that leaves us with no imaginative, affective, or emotional sense of either God's love or God's existence. No effort on our part can again conjure up the feelings and images we once had about God and the security we once felt within ourselves about our faith and religious beliefs. The heavens empty and inside ourselves we feel agnostic, as if God didn't exist, and we are no longer able to create an image of God that feels real to us. We become helpless to generate a sense of God inside ourselves.

But that's precisely the beginning of real faith. In that darkness, when we have nothing left, when we feel there is no God, God can begin to flow into us in a pure way. Because our interior religious faculties are paralyzed we can no longer manipulate our experience of God, fudge it, project ourselves into it, or use it to rationalize divine permission for our own actions. Real faith begins at the exact point where our atheistic critics think it ends, in darkness and emptiness, in religious impotence, in our powerlessness to influence how God flows into us.

We see this clearly in the life of Mother Teresa. As seen in her diaries, for the first twenty-six years of her life she had a deeply felt, imaginative, affective sense of God in her life. She lived with a rocklike certainty about God's existence and God's love. But at age twenty-seven, while praying on a train one day, it was as if someone turned off the switch that connected her to God. In her imagination and her feelings, the heavens emptied. God, as she had known him in her mind and feelings, disappeared.

But we know the rest of the story: She lived out the next sixty years of her life in a faith that truly was rock-solid. She lived out a dedicated, selfless commitment that would strip from even the strongest atheistic critic the power to make the accusation that her religious experience was selfish projection, or that her practice of religion was not essentially pure. In her religious darkness, God was able to flow into her in essential purity—unlike for so many of us, whose faith lives are clearly self-serving and belie a belief that we are listening to God and not to ourselves.

Even Jesus, in his humanity, had to undergo this darkness, as is evident in the Garden of Gethsemane and his cry of abandonment on the cross. After his agony in Gethsemane, we are told that an angel came and strengthened him. Why, we might ask, didn't the angel come earlier, when seemingly he most needed the help? God's assistance couldn't come until he was completely spent in terms of his own strength; his humanity wouldn't have let the divine flow in purely but would have inserted itself into the experience. He had to be completely spent of his own strength before the divine could truly and purely flow in. It is the same way for us.

Dark nights of the soul are needed to wash us clean because only then can the angel come to help us.

The Difference Between Faith and Notions About Faith

When Friedrich Nietzsche declared that "God is dead" he added a question: Who gave us the sponge to wipe away the entire horizon?

I often ask that question because just in my own lifetime

there has been an unprecedented decline in the number of people who go to church regularly and, more recently, an equally unprecedented spike in the number of people who claim to have lost their faith completely; when asked about their religious affiliation on a census form, they answer with the word "None."

The latter group has essentially doubled in the last twenty years, and today in Canada and the United States makes up over 30 percent of the population. The numbers are much the same for Western Europe and other secularized parts of the world.

But have these individuals really lost their faith? When they use the word "None" to refer to their religious beliefs, they generally explain that with phrases to this effect: "I just no longer believe." "It doesn't make sense to me anymore." "I've lost faith in religion and the church." "I can't pretend any longer." "I've lost my faith in those beliefs." "I'm not sure whether or not I believe in God."

What is common among all these phrases is the concept of "believing" or "belief": "I just no longer believe." But is ceasing to believe in something the same thing as losing our faith? Not necessarily. To stop believing in a set of faith propositions doesn't necessarily equate with losing our faith. Indeed, the loss of our belief system is often the condition for a purified faith.

How is belief different from faith? In everyday parlance, to say that we believe something to be true means that we are able to square that truth with our imagination; that is, we are able to somehow circumscribe it imaginatively so that it makes sense to us. Conversely, if we cannot picture how something might make sense, then it is a short step to say that it isn't true. Our beliefs are predicated on what we can square with our imagination and our thinking.

But many of the objects of our faith are, in essence and by definition, unimaginable, ineffable, and beyond conceptualization. To say that we can't believe this or that when it comes to our faith is generally more an indication of the limitation of our imagination and our rational powers than it is indicative of the loss of faith. I believe that we are much more agnostic about our beliefs than we are agnostic about God, and this isn't a loss of faith.

Faith is deeper than belief, and it is not always something we can picture imaginatively inside our minds. Take, for instance, a number of the articles in the Apostles' Creed: It is impossible to imagine them as true in terms of picturing them as real. They are real, but our images of them are only icons. That is true too of many articles within our Christian creed and many of our written doctrines of faith. As expressed, they are merely images and words that point us toward something that we cannot imagine because it is beyond imagination.

For example, the first thing that always needs to be said about God is that God is ineffable; that is, God is beyond all conceptualization, beyond all imaginings, beyond being pictured, and beyond being captured in any adequate way by language. This is also true for our understanding of Christ as the Second Person in the Trinity. Jesus was God's son, but how can that be imagined or pictured? It can't be. How can God, who is one, be three? This isn't mathematics; it's mystery, something that cannot be imaginatively circumscribed. Yet we believe it, and millions and millions of people for two thousand years have risked their lives and their souls on its truth without being able to picture it imaginatively. Faith is a knowing of something that, because of its magnitude and infinity, cannot be adequately pictured in terms of an imaginative construct. Our words about it express our beliefs and those words point to the reality, but they are not the reality.

To reject a specific piece of art does not mean we reject beauty. So when someone says, "I can no longer believe this," he is in effect rejecting a set of propositions, a set of particular icons, and a theory of art (a theology) rather than actually rejecting belief in God, and he is rejecting it precisely because he cannot imaginatively picture something that in fact cannot be pictured.

It has been said that "atheist" is just another name for someone who cannot get metaphor. Perhaps that's too simple, but it does suggest that rejecting a set of theological propositions is not the same thing as losing one's faith.

The Search for God Outside Explicit Faith

"To whom else can we go? You have the message of eternal life." Peter says these words to Jesus. But they are spoken in a very conflicted context: Jesus had just said something that upset and offended his audience, and the Gospels tell us that everyone walked away grumbling that what Jesus was teaching was "intolerable." Jesus then turns to his apostles and asks them, "Do you want to walk away too?" Peter answers, "To whom else can we go?" But that's more a statement of stoic resignation than an actual question.

His words function at two levels. On the surface, they express an unwanted humility and helplessness that sometimes beset us all: "I have no alternative! I'm so invested in this relationship that now I have no other options. I'm stuck with this!" That's a humble place to stand, and anyone who has ever given himself or herself over in an authentic commitment will eventually stand on that place, knowing that he or she no longer has another practical choice.

But those words also express a much deeper quandary—namely, Where can I find meaning if I cannot find it in faith in God? All of us have at some point asked ourselves that question. If I didn't believe in God and had no faith or religion, what would give meaning to my life?

Where can we go if we no longer have an explicit faith in God? A lot of places, it seems. I think immediately of so many attractive stoics who have wrestled with this question and found solace in various forms of what Albert Camus would call "metaphysical rebellion" or in the kind of Epicureanism that Nikos Kazantzakis advocates in *Zorba the Greek*. There's a stoicism that offers its own kind of salvation by drawing life and meaning simply from fighting chaos and disease for no other reason than that these cause suffering and are an affront to life, just as there is an Epicureanism that meaningfully grounds life in elemental pleasure. There are, it would seem, different kinds of saints.

There are also different kinds of immortality. For some, meaning outside an explicit faith is found in leaving a lasting legacy on this earth, having children, achieving something monumental, or becoming a household name. Poets, writers, artists, and artisans often have their own place to find meaning outside explicit faith. For them, creativity and beauty can be ends in themselves: art for art's sake. Creativity itself can seem enough.

And there are still others for whom deep meaning is found simply in being good for its own sake and in being honest for its own sake. There's also virtue for virtue's sake, and virtue is indeed its own reward. Simply living an honest and generous life can provide sufficient meaning with which to walk through life.

So it appears that there are places to go outside explicit faith where one can find deep meaning. But is this really so? Can anything other than faith and God really quiet the restless fires within us?

Yes, there are things that can do that, but all of them—fighting chaos, curing diseases, having children, living for others, building things, inventing things, achieving goals, or simply living honest and generous lives—leave us, in an inchoate way, radiating the transcendental properties of God and working alongside God to bring life and order to the world. How so?

Christian theology tells us that God is One, True, Good, and Beautiful. And so, when an artist gives herself over to creating beauty, when a couple has a child, when scientists work to find cures for various diseases, when artisans make an artifact, when builders build, when teachers teach, when parents parent, when athletes play a game, when manual laborers labor, when administrators administrate, when people just for the sake of integrity itself live in honesty and generosity, and, yes, even when hedonists drink deeply of earthly pleasure, they are, all of them, whether they have explicit faith or not, acting in some faith because they are putting their trust in either the oneness, truth, goodness, or beauty of God.

"Lord, to whom else can we go? You have the message of eternal life." Well, it seems that there are places to go and many go there. But these aren't necessarily empty places that are wrong and self-destructive, as is sometimes suggested by misguided spiritual literature. There are, of course, such places, spiritual dead ends; but, more generally, as we can see simply by looking at the amount of positive energy, love, creativity, generosity, and honesty that still fill our world, those places where people are seeking God outside explicit faith still have them meeting God.

CHAPTER SIX

Wrestling with God

What's madness but nobility of soul / At odds with circumstance?

—THEODORE ROETHKE

Thy Will Be Changed!

In his memoir, *Report to Greco*, Nikos Kazantzakis shares this story: As a young man, he spent a summer in a monastery during which he had a series of conversations with an old monk. One day he asked the old monk, "Do you still wrestle with the devil, Father Makários?" The old monk replied, "Not any longer, my child. I have grown old now, and he has grown old with me. He doesn't have the strength. . . . I wrestle with God."

There's a lot contained in that remark—"I wrestle with

God." Among other things, it suggests that the struggles in later life can be very different from those of our younger years. In the normal scheme of things, we spend the first half of our lives struggling with sensuality, greed, and sexuality, and spend the last half struggling with anger and forgiveness—and that anger is often, however unconsciously, focused on God. In the end, our real struggle isn't with regret. It is with God.

But wrestling with God has another aspect. It invites us to a certain kind of prayer. Prayer isn't meant to be a simple acquiescence to God's will. It's meant to be an acquiescence, yes, but a mature acquiescence, one come to at the end of a long struggle.

We see this in the prayers of the great figures in the scriptures: Abraham, Moses, the apostles, Jesus. Abraham argues with God and initially talks him out of destroying Sodom; Moses at first resists his call, protesting that his brother is better suited for the job; the apostles excuse themselves for a long time before finally putting their lives on the line; and Jesus gives himself over in the Garden of Gethsemane only after first begging his Father for a reprieve. As Rabbi Abraham Heschel, one of the leading Jewish philosophers and theologians of the twentieth century, puts it, from Abraham through Jesus we see how the great figures of our faith are not in the habit of easily saying "Thy will be done!" but often, for a while at least, counter God's invitation with "Thy will be changed!"

Struggling with God's will and offering resistance to what it calls us to can be a bad thing, but it can also be a mature form of prayer. The book of Genesis describes an incident where Jacob wrestled with a spirit for a whole night and in the morning that spirit turned out to be God. What a perfect icon for prayer! A human being and God, wrestling in the dust of this earth! Doesn't that accurately describe the human struggle?

We would do well to integrate this concept of wrestling with God into our understanding of faith and prayer. We honor neither ourselves nor the scriptures when we make things too simple. Human will doesn't bend easily, nor should it, and the heart has complexities that need to be respected, even as we try to rein in its more possessive longings. God, who built us, understands this and is up to the task of wrestling with us and our resistance.

The classical mystics speak of something they call "being bold with God." This "boldness," they suggest, comes not at the beginning of the spiritual journey, but more toward the end of it, when, after a long period of fidelity, we are intimate enough with God to precisely be "bold," as friends who have known each other for a long time have a right to be. That's a valuable insight: After you have been friends with someone for a long time, you can be comfortable with expressing your needs to him or her, and in the context of a long, sustained relationship unquestioning reverence is not necessarily a sign of mature intimacy.

Old friends, precisely because they know and trust each other, can risk a boldness in their friendship that those in a younger, less mature friendship avoid expressing.

That is also true in our relationship with God. God expects that at some point we will kick against his will and offer some resistance. But we should lay out our hearts in honesty. Jesus did.

God certainly expects some resistance. As Nikos Kazantzakis puts it: The struggle between God and man breaks out in everyone, together with the longing for reconciliation. Most often this struggle is unconscious and short-lived. A weak soul does not have the endurance to resist the flesh for very long. It grows heavy, becomes flesh itself, and the contest ends. But among responsible persons who keep their eyes riveted day and night upon the supreme duty, the conflict between flesh and spirit breaks out mercilessly and may last until death. The stronger the soul and the flesh, the more fruitful the struggle and the richer the final harmony. The spirit wants to have to wrestle with flesh that is strong and full of resistance. It is a carnivorous bird that is incessantly hungry; it eats flesh and, by assimilating it, makes it disappear.

The Ineffability of God

British theologian Nicholas Lash, in a deeply insightful essay on God and unbelief, suggests that the God that atheists reject is often simply an idol of their own imaginations:

> We need do no more than notice that most of our contemporaries still find it "obvious" that atheism is not only possible, but widespread and that, both intellectually and ethically, it has much to commend it. This might be plausible if being an atheist were a matter of not believing that there exists "a person without a body" who is "eternal, free, able to do anything, knows everything" and is "the proper object of human worship and obedience, the creator and sustainer of the universe." If, however, by "God" we mean the mystery, announced in Christ, breathing all things out of nothing into peace, then all things have to do with God in every move and fragment of their being, whether they notice this and suppose it to be so or not. Atheism, if it means deciding not to have anything to do with God, is thus self-contradictory and, if successful, self-destructive.*

---

* Nicholas Lash, "Among Strangers and Friends," in *Finding God in All Things: Essays in Honor of Michael J. Buckley, S.J.*, ed. Michael J. Himes and Stephen J. Pope (New York: Crossroad, 1996), 57.

Lash's insight is, I believe, very important for our understanding of our own faith. The first thing that Christianity defines dogmatically about God is that God is ineffable—that is, that it is impossible to conceptualize God and that all of our language about God is more inaccurate than accurate. That isn't just an abstract dogma. Our failure to understand this, perhaps more than anything else, is the reason why we struggle with faith and struggle to not fudge its demands. What's at issue here?

All of us, naturally, try to form some picture of God and try to imagine God's existence. The problem when we try to do this is that we end up in one of two places, both not good.

On the one hand, we often end up with an image of God as some kind of superman, a person like ourselves, except wonderfully superior to us in every way. We picture God as a superhero, divine, all-knowing, and all-powerful, but still ultimately like us, capable of being imagined and pictured, someone whom we can circumscribe, put a face to, and count. While this is natural and unavoidable, it always leaves us, no matter how sincere we are, with an idol, a God created in our own image and likeness, and consequently a God who can easily and rightly be rejected by atheism.

On the other hand, sometimes when we try to form a picture of God and imagine God's existence, something else happens: We come up dry and empty, unable to either picture God or imagine God's existence. We then end up either in some form of atheism or afraid to examine our faith because we have unconsciously internalized atheism's belief that faith is naive and cannot stand up to the hard questions.

When this happens to us, when we try to imagine God's existence and come up empty, that failure is not one of faith but of our imagination. We are living not so much inside atheism as inside God's ineffability, inside the "cloud of unknowing," the "dark night of the soul." We aren't atheists. We just feel like we are. It's not that God doesn't exist or has disappeared. It's rather that God's ineffability has put God outside our imaginative capacities. Our minds are overmatched. God is still real, still there, but our finite imaginations are coming up empty trying to picture infinite reality, tantamount to what happens when we try to imagine the highest number to which it is possible to count. The infinite cannot be circumscribed by the imagination. It has no floor and it has no ceiling, no beginning and no end. The human imagination cannot deal with that.

God is infinite and thus, by definition, unimaginable and impossible to conceptualize. That's also true for God's existence. It cannot be pictured. However, the fact that we cannot imagine God is very different from saying that we cannot know God. God can be known, even if not imagined. How?

We all know many things that we cannot imagine, conceptualize, or articulate. Inside us there is something the mystics call "dark knowledge"—namely, an inchoate, intuitive, gut sense within which we know and understand beyond what we can picture and give words to. And this isn't some exotic, paranormal talent that fortune-tellers claim to have—just the opposite: it's our bedrock, that solid foundation we touch in our most sincere and deepest moments, that place inside us where when we are at our best we ground our lives.

God is ineffable, unimaginable, and beyond conception and language. Our faith lets us bracket this for a while and lets us picture God as some idolized superhero. But eventually that well runs dry, and our finite minds are left to know the infinite only in darkness, without images, and our finite hearts are left to feel infinite love only inside a dark trust.

God's Inexhaustibility

Many of us, I am sure, have been inspired by the movie *Of Gods and Men*, which tells the story of a group of Trappist monks who, after making a painful decision not to flee from the violence in Algeria in the 1990s, are eventually martyred by Islamic extremists in 1996. Recently, I was much inspired by reading the diaries of one of those monks, Christophe Lebreton. *Born from the Gaze of God: The Tibhirine Journal of a Martyr Monk* chronicles the last three years of his life and gives us an insight into his, and his community's, decision to remain in Algeria in the face of almost certain death.

In one of his journal entries, Christophe shares how in this situation of hatred and threat, caught between Islamic extremists on one side and a corrupt government on the other, in seeking ground for hope, he draws upon a poem, "The Well," by the French poet Jean-Claude Renard:

> *But how can we affirm it's already too late*
> *to fulfill the desire—*
> *so patient does the gift remain;*
> *and when always, perhaps, something or*
> *someone says, from the depth of silence and*
> *nakedness,*
> *that an ineffable fire continues to dig in us*
> *beneath wastelands peopled by thorns*
> *a well that nothing exhausts.*
> *A well that nothing exhausts.**

Perhaps that is the real basis for hope.

For all of us there are times in life when we seem to lose hope, when we look at the world or at ourselves and, consciously or unconsciously, think: "It's too late! This has

---

* This is taken from Christophe Lebreton, *Born from the Gaze of God: The Tibhirine Journal of a Martyr Monk (1993–1996)* (Collegeville, Minn.: Liturgical Press, 2014), 85.

gone too far! Nothing can redeem this! All the chances to change this have been used up! It's hopeless!"

But is this natural, depressive feeling in fact a loss of hope? Not necessarily. Indeed, it is precisely when we feel this way, when we have succumbed to the feeling that we have exhausted all of our chances, that hope can arrive and replace its counterfeits: wishful thinking and natural optimism. What is hope?

We generally confuse hope with either wishful thinking or natural optimism, both of which have little to do with hope. Wishful thinking has no foundation. We can wish to win a lottery or to have the body of a world-class athlete, but that wish has no reality upon which to draw. It's pure fantasy. Optimism, for its part, is based upon natural temperament and also has little to do with hope. In *Hope Without Optimism*, the literary theorist Terry Eagleton suggests rather cynically that optimism is simply a natural temperament and an enslaving one at that: "You are chained to your cheerfulness like a slave to his oar." Moreover, he asserts that the optimist's monochrome glaze over the world differs from pessimism only by being monochromatically rosy instead of monochromatically gray. Hope isn't a wish or a mood; it is a perspective on life that needs to be grounded on a sufficient reality. What is that sufficient reality?

Jim Wallis says that our hope should not be grounded on what we see on the world news each night, because that news constantly changes and can be so negative on any given night that it gives us little basis for hope. He's right. Whether the world seems better or worse on a particular evening is hardly sufficient cause for us to trust that in the end all will be well. Things might change drastically the next night.

Pierre Teilhard de Chardin, who perennially protested that he was a man of hope rather than optimism, once suggested in an answer to a question that there are two sufficient reasons for hope. Asked what would happen if we blew up the world with an atomic bomb, he replied that it would set things back a few million years, but God's plan for the earth would still come about. Why? Because Christ promised it and, in the resurrection, God shows that he has the power to deliver on that promise. Hope is based upon God's promise and God's power.

But there is still another reason for our hope, something else that grounds it and gives us sufficient reason to live in trust that eventually all will be well—namely, God's inexhaustibility. Underneath and beneath us and our universe is *a well that nothing exhausts.*

And this is what we so often forget or slim down to the limited size of our own hearts and imaginations: God is a prodigal God, almost unimaginable in the scope of physical creation, a God who has created and is still creating billions upon billions of universes. Moreover, this prodigal God, so beyond our imagination in creativity, is, as has been revealed to us by Jesus, equally unimaginable in patience and mercy. There is never an end to our number of chances. There is no limit to God's patience. There is nothing that can ever exhaust the divine well.

It's never too late! God's creativity and mercy are inexhaustible.

God's Powerlessness

The French novelist and essayist Léon Bloy once made this comment about God's power in our world: "God seems to have condemned himself until the end of time not to exercise any immediate right of a master over a servant or a king over a subject. We can do what we want. He will defend himself only by his patience and his beauty."

God defends himself only by his patience and his beauty! How true. And how significant for our understanding of power.

The way we understand power is invariably bound up with how we see power exercised in our world. Our world understands power precisely as a force that can lord it over others and compel them to obey. In our world, power is understood to be real only when it can forcibly assert itself to make others obey it. For us, strong people have power, political rulers have power, economic systems have power, billionaires have power, the rich and the famous have power, muscular bodies have power, and the playground bully has power—power that can make you buckle under, one way or the other.

But such a notion of power is adolescent and superficial. Power that can make you buckle under is only one kind of power and ultimately not the most transformative kind. Real power is moral. Real power is the power of truth, beauty, and patience. Paradoxically, real power generally looks helpless. If you put a powerfully muscled athlete, the CEO of a powerful corporation, a playground bully, an Academy Award–winning movie star, and a baby into the same room, who has the most power? Ultimately, it's the baby. At the end of the day, the baby's helplessness over-powers physical muscle, economic muscle, and charismatic muscle. Babies cleanse a room morally: they do exorcisms; even the most callous watch their language around a baby.

That's the kind of power God revealed in the incar-nation. Against almost all human expectation, God was born into this world, not as Superman or Superstar, but as a baby, helpless to care for his own needs. And that's how God is still essentially present in our lives. The Pulitzer Prize–winning writer Annie Dillard suggests that this is how we forever find God in our lives, as a helpless infant lying in the straw whom we need to pick up, nurture, and provide with human flesh.

She's right, and her insight, like that of Léon Bloy, has huge implications for how we understand both God's power in our lives and God's seeming silence in our lives.

When we examine the biblical account of Adam and Eve and original sin, we see that the primary motivation for eating the apple was their desire to somehow grasp at divinity, to become like God. They wanted godlike power. But they, like us, badly misunderstood what makes for genuine power. Saint Paul shows us the antithesis of that in how he describes Jesus in the well-known Christological hymn in the Epistle to the Philippians. Paul writes there that Jesus did not deem equality with God something to be grasped at, but rather that he emptied himself of that power to become helpless, trusting that this emptying and helplessness would ultimately be the most transformative power of all. Jesus submitted to helplessness to become truly powerful.

That insight can shed light on how we understand God's apparent absence in our world. How might we comprehend what is often called "the silence of God"? Where was God during the Holocaust? Where is God during natural disasters that kill thousands of people? Where is God when senseless accidents and illnesses take the lives of countless persons? Why doesn't God forcefully intervene?

God is present and intervening in all these situations, but not in the way we ordinarily understand presence, power, and intervention. God is present the way beauty is present, in the way a helpless, innocent newborn is present, and in the way truth as a moral agent is always present. God is never silent because beauty, innocence, helplessness, and truth are never silent. They're always present and intervening, but unlike ordinary human power, they're present in a way that is completely nonmanipulative and fully respectful of your freedom. God's power, like that of a newborn, like the power of beauty itself, fully respects you by never forcing itself on you.

When we look at the struggles within our world and our private lives, it often seems like divine power is forever being trumped by human power. As the cartoon character Ziggy likes to put it, "the poor are still getting clobbered in our world." Like David standing with just a boy's slingshot before Goliath, a giant who looks overpowering in terms of muscle and iron, and just like the apostles being asked to set five little loaves of bread and two tiny fish before a crowd of five thousand, God always looks underwhelming in our world.

But we know how these stories end.

God's Nonviolence

In his deeply insightful book *Violence Unveiled*, Gil Bailie takes us through a remarkable section of the diaries of Captain James Cook, the famed British scientist and explorer. Visiting the island of Tahiti in 1777, Cook was taken one day by a local tribal chief to witness a ritual where a man was sacrificed as an offering to the god Eatooa. The man was being sacrificed in the hope that this particular god would give the tribe some assistance in an upcoming war. Cook, though friendly to the local people, could not conceal his detestation for what he considered both a barbaric and superstitious act. In a conversation with the tribal chief afterward, Cook told him, through an interpreter, that in England they would hang a man for such brutality.

Cook found the idea of killing someone to appease God to be abhorrent. Yet, as the great irony inside this story makes clear, we have never stopped killing people in God's name; we have only changed the nomenclature. They called it human sacrifice; we call it capital punishment. In either case, someone dies because we feel that God needs and wants this death for some divine reason.

All peoples, right up to this day, have always done violence in God's name, believing that the violence is not only justified but is in fact necessitated by God. God, it is argued, needs us to do this violence in his name. For this reason, ancient cultures often offered human sacrifice. During the medieval ages, the Christian church, believing that God wanted us to kill people who were in doctrinal error, conducted the Inquisition. Today we see a new form of this in a number of extremist Islamic groups who believe that God wants infidels of all kinds put to death for the sake of religious purity.

We have forever justified killing and other forms of violence in God's name, often pointing to scriptural texts that seemingly show God as ordering violence in his name. But in this, we have been wrong. Despite a number of texts that on the surface seem to indicate that God is ordering violence (but that are really archetypal and anthropomorphic in nature and do not justify that interpretation), we see, if we read the Bible from beginning to end, a progressive revelation (or at least a progressive realization on our part) of the nonviolence of God, a revelation that ends in Jesus, who reveals a God of radical nonviolence. Our faulty idea of the God of the Old Testament who seemingly orders the extermination of whole peoples is indeed primitive and superstitious when placed beside the concept of the Father of Jesus, who sends his Son into the world as a defenseless infant and then lets him die helpless before a mocking crowd. The God whom Jesus reveals is devoid of all violence and asks that we no longer do violence in God's name.

To offer just one example: In the Gospel of John (8:2–11), we see the story of a woman who has been caught in adultery. A pious crowd brings her to Jesus and tells him that they have caught her in an act for which she needs to be stoned to death, according to the orders of Moses (their primary interpreter of God's will). Jesus, for his part, says nothing; instead, he bends down and begins to write on the ground with his finger. Then, looking up, he tells them, "Let the person among you without sin cast the first stone!" Then he bends down and writes for a second time with his finger. Unbelievably, they get the message and put down their stones and go away.

What has happened here? The key for interpretation is Jesus's gesture of writing on the ground with his finger. Who writes with his finger? Who writes twice? God does. And what God writes with his finger and writes twice are the Ten Commandments, and he had to write them twice because Moses "broke" them the first time. As he was coming down the mountain, carrying the tablets, Moses caught the people in the very act of committing idolatry; gripped in a fever of religious and moral fervor, he broke the tablets of stone on the golden calf and the heads of the people. Moses was the first person to break the commandments, and he broke them physically, thinking violence needed to be done for God's cause. Having broken them, he needed to go up the mountain a second time; before rewriting them, God gave Moses a stern message: Don't stone people with the commandments! Don't do violence in my name! The people who wanted to stone the woman caught in adultery understood Jesus's gesture. Their divine interpreter, Moses, had it wrong.

Too often, though, we are still stoning people with the commandments, falsely believing that God wants this violence.

God's Prodigal Character

Nearly two decades ago, Barbara Kingsolver wrote a book entitled *Prodigal Summer*. It tells the story of a young woman who gets pregnant during a summer within which everything seems to be dangerously fertile. From the plants, insects, and animals to the people, everything seems to be teeming with fecundity, overactive, overabundant in seed. Life seems to be bursting forth everywhere. The title of the book is a good metaphor for what she describes, a summer overabundant in fertility.

Nature is like that, teeming with everything, prodigal, fertile, overabundant, wasteful. Why else do we have 90 percent more brain cells than we need and why else is nature scattering billions of seeds, of virtually everything, all over the planet every second?

And if life is so prodigal, what does this say about God, its author?

God, as we see in both nature and the scriptures (and know from experience), is overgenerous, overlavish, overextravagant, overprodigious, overrich, and overpatient. If nature, the scriptures, and experience are to be believed, God is the absolute antithesis of everything that is stingy, miserly, frugal, narrowly calculating, or sparing in what it doles out. God is prodigal.

Dictionaries define "prodigal" as "wastefully extravagant and lavishly abundant." That certainly describes the God that Jesus incarnates and reveals.

We see this in the parable of the sower. God, the sower, goes out to sow and he scatters his seed generously, almost wastefully, everywhere—on the road, among the rocks, among the thorns, on bad soil, and on rich soil. No farmer would ever do this. Who would waste seed on soil that can never produce a harvest? God, it seems, doesn't ask that question but simply keeps scattering his seed everywhere, overgenerously, without calculating whether it is a good investment or not in terms of return. And, it seems, God has an infinite number of seeds to scatter, perpetually, everywhere. God is prodigious beyond imagination.

Among other things, this speaks of God's infinite riches, love, and patience. For us, there is both a huge challenge and a huge consolation in that. The challenge, of course, is to respond to the infinite number of invitations that God scatters on our path from minute to minute. The consolation is that, no matter how many of God's invitations we ignore, there will always be an infinite number of others. No matter how many we've already ignored or turned down, there are new ones awaiting us each minute. When we've gone through thirty-nine days of Lent without praying or changing our lives, there's still a fortieth day to respond. When we've ignored a thousand invitations, there's still another one waiting. God is prodigal; so are the chances God gives us.

Sister Margaret Halaska once captured this wonderfully in a poem she entitled "Covenant":

The Father knocks at my door, seeking a home
for his son:
Rent is cheap, I say.
I don't want to rent. I want to buy, says God.
I'm not sure I want to sell,
but you might come in to look around.
I think I will, says God.
I might let you have a room or two.
I like it, says God. I'll take the two.
You might decide to give me more some day.
I can wait, says God.
I'd like to give you more,
but it's a bit difficult. I need some space for me.
I know, says God, but I'll wait. I like what I
see.
Hm, maybe I can let you have another room.
I really don't need that much.
Thanks, says God, I'll take it. I like what I
see.
I'd like to give you the whole house
but I'm not sure—
Think on it, says God. I wouldn't put you out.
Your house would be mine and my son would
live in it.

You'd have more space than you'd ever had
  before.
I don't understand at all.
I know, says God, but I can't tell you about
  that.
You'll have to discover it for yourself.
That can only happen if you let him have the
  whole house.
A bit risky, I say.
Yes, says God, but try me.
I'm not sure—
I'll let you know.
*I can wait, says God. I like what I see.**

If we look back on our lives and are truly honest, we have to admit that of all the invitations that God has sent us, we've probably accepted and acted on only a fraction of them. There have been countless times we've turned away from an invitation. But that's the beauty and wonder of God's richness. God is not a petty creator, and creation is not a cheap machine with barely enough energy and resources to keep it going. God and nature are prodigal. That's plain everywhere. Millions and millions of life-giving seeds blow everywhere in the world, and we need

---

* Margaret Halaska, OSF, *Review for Religious.* May/June 1981.

only to pick up a few to become spiritually pregnant, fecund, capable of newness, maturity, and producing life.

God's Exuberance

It's funny where you can learn a lesson and catch a glimpse of the divine. Recently, in a grocery store, I witnessed this incident:

A young girl, probably around sixteen, came into the store with two other girls her own age. She picked up a grocery basket and began to walk down the aisle, not knowing that a second basket was stuck to the one she was carrying. At a point the inevitable happened: the basket stuck to hers released and crashed to the floor with a loud bang, startling her and all of us around her. What was her reaction? She burst into laughter, exuding a joy-filled delight at being so startled. For her the surprise of the falling basket was not an irritation but a gift, an unexpected humor happily fracturing our drab routine.

If that had happened to me, given how I'm habitually in a hurry and easily irritated by anything that disrupts my agenda, I would probably have responded with a silent expletive rather than with laughter. The contrast made me think: In such a moment, a young girl who probably isn't going to church and probably isn't much concerned about matters of faith, but who, in this moment, is wonderfully radiating the energy of God, while I, a vowed religious, overserious priest, church minister, and spiritual writer, in such a moment too often radiate the antithesis of God's energy.

But is this true? Does God really burst into laughter at falling grocery baskets? Doesn't God ever get irritated? What is God's real nature?

God is the unconditional love and forgiveness that Jesus reveals, but God is also the energy that lies at the base of everything that is. And that energy, as is evident in both creation and the scriptures, is, at its root, creative, prodigal, robust, joy-filled, playful, and exuberant. If you want to know what God is like, look at the natural exuberance of children, the friskiness of a young puppy, the robust, playful energy of young people, and the spontaneous laughter of a sixteen-year-old when she is startled by a falling basket. And to see God's prodigal character, we might look at the billions and billions of planets that surround us. The energy of God is abundant and exuberant.

Then what about the cross? Doesn't it, more than anything else, reveal God's nature? Isn't it what shows us God? Isn't suffering the innate and necessary route to maturity and sanctity? So isn't there a contradiction between what Jesus reveals about the nature of God in his crucifixion and what the scriptures and nature reveal about God's exuberance?

While there's clearly a paradox here, there's no contradiction. First, the tension we see between the cross and exuberance is already seen in the person and teachings of Jesus. Jesus scandalized his contemporaries in opposite ways: both his capacity to willingly give up his life and the things of this world and his capacity to enjoy life and drink in its God-given pleasures scandalized them. His contemporaries weren't able to walk with him while he carried the cross and they weren't able to walk with him either as he ate and drank without guilt and felt only gift and gratitude when a woman anointed his feet with expensive perfume.

Moreover, the joy and exuberance that lie at the root of God's nature are not to be confused with the bravado we crank up at parties, carnival, and Mardi Gras. What's experienced at these events is not actual delight but a numbing of the brain and senses induced by frenzied excess. This doesn't radiate the exuberance of God, nor does it radiate the powerful exuberance that sits inside us, waiting to burst forth. Carnival is mostly an attempt to keep depression at bay. As Charles Taylor astutely points out, we invented carnival because our natural exuberance doesn't find enough outlets within our daily lives, so we ritualize certain occasions and seasons where we can, for a time, imprison our rationality, and release our exuberance, as one would free a caged animal. We can open the valve of mindless revelry to let off steam, but it is not the ideal way to release our natural exuberance.

When I was a child, my parents would often warn me

about the false exuberance of wild partying, phony laughter, and carnival. They summed this up in a little axiom: After the laughter, come the tears! They were right, but their maxim applies only to the kind of laughter that we tend to crank up at parties to keep depression at bay. The cross, however, reverses my parents' axiom: After the tears, comes the laughter! Only after the cross is our joy genuine. Only after the cross will our exuberance express the genuine delight we once felt when we were little, and only then will our exuberance truly radiate the energy of God.

Jesus promises us that if we take up his cross, God will reward us with an exuberance that no one can ever take from us.

God's Flavor

All things considered, I believe that I grew up with a relatively healthy concept of God. The God of my youth, the God of my catechism, was not unduly punishing, arbitrary, or judgmental. He was omnipresent, so that all of our sins were noticed and noted, but, at the end of the day, he was fair, loving, personally concerned for each individual, and wonderfully protective, to the point of providing each of us with a personal guardian angel. That God gave me permission to live without too much fear and without any particularly crippling religious neuroses.

But that only gets you so far in life. Not having an unhealthy notion of God doesn't necessarily mean that your conception of God is a particularly healthy one. The God I was raised to worship was not overly stern and judgmental, but he wasn't very joyous, playful, witty, or humorous either. In particular, he wasn't sexual and had an especially vigilant and uncompromising eye in that area. He was gray, a bit dour, and not very joyous to be around. You had to be solemn and reverent in his presence. I remember the assistant director at our Oblate novitiate telling us that there is no recorded incident, ever, of Jesus having laughed. Under such a God you had permission to be essentially healthy, but, to the extent that you took him seriously, you still walked through life less than fully robust.

Then, a generation ago, there was a strong reaction in many churches and in the culture at large to this concept of God. Popular theology and spirituality set out to correct it, sometimes with an undue vigor. What they presented instead was a laughing Jesus and a dancing God. This new depiction was not without its value, but it still left us begging for a deeper literature about God's nature and what that might mean for us in terms of a healthy relationship with him.

That literature won't be easy to write, not just because God is ineffable, but because God's energy is also ineffable. What is energy? We rarely ask this question because we take energy as something so primal that it cannot be defined but only taken as a given, as self-evident. We see energy as the primal force that lies at the heart of everything that exists, animate and inanimate. Moreover, we feel energy, powerfully, within ourselves. We know energy, we feel energy, but we rarely recognize its origins, its prodigiousness, its joy, its goodness, its effervescence, and its exuberance. We rarely recognize what it tells us about God. What does it tell us?

The first quality of energy is its prodigiousness. It is prodigal beyond our imagination and this speaks something about God. What kind of creator makes billions of throwaway universes? What kind of creator makes trillions upon trillions of species of life, millions of them never to be seen by the human eye? What kind of father or mother has billions of children?

And what does the exuberance in the energy of young children say about our creator? What does their playfulness suggest about what must also lie inside sacred energy? What does the enthusiasm of a young puppy tell us about what's sacred? What do laughter, wit, and irony tell us about God?

No doubt the energy we see around us and feel irrepressibly within us tells us that underneath, before and below everything else, there flows a sacred force, both physical and spiritual, that is at its root joyous, happy, playful, exuberant, effervescent, and deeply personal and loving. That energy is God. That energy speaks of God and that energy tells us why God made us and what kind of permission God is giving us for living out our lives.

When we try to imagine the heart of reality, we might picture things this way: At the very center of everything sit two thrones; on one sits a king and on the other sits a queen, and from these two thrones all energy, all creativity, all power, all love, all nourishment, all joy, all playfulness, all humor, and all beauty issue forth. All images of God are inadequate, but this image hopefully can help us understand that God is perfect masculinity and perfect femininity making perfect love all the time and that from this union issues forth all energy and all creation. Moreover, that energy, at its sacred root, is not just creative, intelligent, personal, and loving; it's also joyous, colorful, witty, playful, humorous, erotic, and exuberant at its very core. To feel it is an invitation to gratitude.

The challenge of our lives is to live inside that energy in a way that honors it and its origins. That means keeping our shoes off before the burning bush as we respect its sacredness, even as we take from it permission to be more robust, free, joyous, humorous, and playful—and especially more grateful.

CHAPTER SEVEN

Wrestling for Faith Within a Complex Culture

We are too late for the gods and too early for Being.

——MARTIN HEIDEGGER

Secularity, a Mixed Bag

We live in a highly secularized culture. Generally, this draws one of three reactions from Christians of all denominations struggling to live out faith in this context.

The first group sees secularity more as an enemy of faith and the churches than as an ally. In their view, secularity is a threat to religion and morality and is, in the name of freedom and open-mindedness, slowly suffocating

Christian freedom. For them, secularity contains within itself a certain tyranny of relativism that can aptly be labeled "post-Christian" and "a culture of death."

The second group simply accommodates itself to the culture without a lot of critical reflection either way. They adjust faith to culture and culture to faith as suits their situation. For them, faith becomes largely a cultural heritage, an ethos more than a religion, though this is not as much of a blind sellout as it first appears. Deeper struggles go on beneath, prompted not just by the soul's perennial questions but also by the Judeo-Christian genes inside the DNA of both the culture and the individual. So these individuals selectively take values from both the Judeo-Christian tradition and the secular culture and blend them into a new marriage, seemingly without a lot of religious anxiety.

The third group has a more nuanced approach: Religious thinkers such as Charles Taylor, Louis Dupré, Kathleen Norris, and, a generation earlier, Karl Rahner see secularity as a mixed bag, a culture of both life and death, progressing and purifying moral and religious values, even as it is losing ground morally and religiously in other ways. Of major importance in this view is the idea that secularity is the child of Judaism and Christianity. Judeo-Christianity, at least for the most part, gave birth to René Descartes, the principles of the Enlightenment, the American Revolution, and the French Revolution, and thus to democracy, the separation of church and state, and the essential principle that undergirds secularity—namely, that we agree to organize public life on the principle of rational consensus rather than divine authority (allowing, of course, for divine authority to influence rational consensus).

In this view, the opposite of secularity is not the church but the Taliban or any other view that public life should be governed by divine authority irrespective of rational consensus. Secularity then is more our child than our enemy. However, if that is true, why is secularity often so bitter and overly critical in its attitude toward the Christian churches? This can seem like a contradiction, but secularity can be anti-Christian for the same reason that adolescents can be bitter and overly critical toward their own parents—namely, because adolescence is often immature and grandiose. But an immature, grandiose adolescent isn't a bad person, just an unfinished one.

Viewing secularity from this perspective, it is equally important to highlight the moral and religious ground that has been both lost and gained. For example, look at a highly secularized culture like that of the Netherlands: It is very weak in church attendance and explicit Christian practice. Abortion, drugs, prostitution, and pornography are tolerated and legal. But it takes care of its poor better than any other society in the world, and is recognized for its emphasis on generosity, peace, and the equality of women. These are not minor religious and moral achievements.

In essence, secularity is not our enemy but our child,

and it carries inside itself both highly generative streams of life and asphyxiating rivulets of death. On the positive side, we can draw a lot of life and joy from its creativity, color, exuberance, and generative energy, often against our own adult propensity for grayness and acedia. We also need to recognize the genuine goodness that we find in most people we meet. In the United States, we reap its stunning benefits—freedom (including the freedom to practice our faith and religion), protection of our rights, privacy, the opportunity for education, wonderful medical care, access to information and technology, wide cultural and recreational opportunities, clean water, and plentiful food.

On the negative side, we need to recognize secularity's elements of death: tolerance of abortion, marginalization of the poor, the itch for euthanasia, lingering racism, widespread sexual irresponsibility, a growing addiction to pornography, and increasing trivialization and superficiality.

As spiritual descendants of René Descartes, we breathe in secularity, a very mixed air, pure and polluted, and we find ourselves torn between hope and fear, comfortable but uneasy, defending secularity even as we are critical of many of its aspects.

Culture Changes Who We Are

A friend of mine shares this story: As a young boy in the 1950s he was struck down with pneumonia. His family lived in a small town that had neither a hospital nor a doctor. His father's job had taken him away from the family for that week. His mother was home alone with no phone and no car. Frightened and completely without resources, she came to his sickbed, knelt beside it, pinned a medal of Saint Thérèse of Lisieux to his pajamas, and prayed to her in words to this effect: "I'm trusting you to make my child better. I'm going to remain kneeling here until his fever breaks."

Both my friend and his mother eventually fell asleep, he in his sickbed and she kneeling beside it. When they woke, his fever had broken.

My friend doesn't share this story to claim that some kind of miracle took place (though who is to judge?). He tells it to make a different point—namely, how his mother, in a situation of fragility and helplessness, dropped to her knees and turned to God as if by natural instinct, and how that kind of a response is no longer our own natural instinct. Very few of us today, faced with a similar situation, would do what his mother did.

Why not? Because our fundamental identity as persons has changed. In *A Secular Age*, Charles Taylor traces how, as our world has grown increasingly secular, we have moved more and more from being porous personalities to becoming buffered personalities.

We have a porous personality when our everyday consciousness stands in anxiety and fear before threats of all kinds (death, illnesses, epidemics, storms, droughts, earthquakes, lightning strikes, wars, evil spirits from other worlds, curses from malevolent persons, bad luck) for which our main and often only defense is power from the other world (God, angels, saints, dead ancestors, benign spirits, fairies, genies). Our personalities are porous when they are made fragile by threats that only powers beyond us can ultimately appease. All human resources within and around us are seen as inadequate and helpless in securing our lives. The natural world is an enchanted world; beneath the surface lurk spirits of all kinds. Coping with life means dealing with not just the physical things of our world but also spirits, good and bad, who, hidden inside and behind things, interfere with life and can bless or curse us. I remember as a child sprinkling myself with holy water for safety during lightning storms. I had a porous personality.

In a buffered personality, everyday consciousness lives inside what Taylor calls "a self-sufficient humanism." Self-sufficient humanism believes that we are essentially adequate to handle the darkness and the threats within life and that there are no ghosts and spirits, good or bad, lurking beneath the surface of things. There is only what we see and that's all—and that's also enough. We don't need help from another world. Someone with a buffered personality doesn't sprinkle herself with holy water during lightning storms; she stands securely behind a safe window and enjoys the free fireworks.

And that lack of fear is not necessarily a bad thing. It's an illusion, of course, but even so, God doesn't want us to live dominated by fear. After all, the word "Gospel" means "good news," not threat. Jesus came into this world to rid us of false fear.

But, with that being said, the belief that we are self-sufficient is still a dangerous illusion and a crippling immaturity. In the end, we are not safe from lightning and disease, no matter how sturdy our windows or good our doctors. To think of ourselves as self-sufficient is naive, an illusion, a choice to live under a pall of enchantment. We are not in control. Moreover, the belief that we are so much more advanced and free than were our grandparents, who were afraid of lightning and pinned religious medals on sick children, is immature. Their fear inspired an important virtue, one that may have been against our own choosing, but it was real. What was that virtue?

The renowned sociologist Robert Bellah once looked at how community and religion tend to thrive inside immigrant communities and challenged us, the post-immigrants, to become "inner-immigrants." That's also true here. We need to get in touch with our "inner porous self"—namely, our deep-down fragility, helplessness, insubstantiality, and lack of self-sufficiency.

The purpose of this virtue is not to instill fear but gratitude. It is only when we realize that we are not in control and that our lives and our safety are in the hands of a great and loving power beyond us that we will bend our knees in gratitude and trust, both when we are joyous and when we are afraid.

Leaving Us Two Churches as Places to Worship

God has given us two churches: one is found everywhere and the other is found at select places. Some of us prefer one of these and struggle with the other, but both are sacred places where God can be found and worshipped.

When most people think of church, they generally think of a building—a cathedral, a shrine, a temple, a synagogue, a mosque—or a holy site. For Roman Catholics, St. Peter's Basilica in Rome or a famous cathedral or their parish church might come to mind. Anglicans and Episcopalians might think of St. Paul's Cathedral in London or their local church. Muslims might imagine Mecca or their neighborhood mosque. These are all privileged holy places where God meets us. But what grounds this concept?

In the book of Genesis we read that Jacob had a dream about a ladder connecting earth to heaven, with angels going up and down. Upon waking from the dream, Jacob realizes that he has had a very privileged experience: witnessing a moment when the gap between heaven and earth was bridged. Not wanting to lose either the experience or the special place, he sets up a stone as a pillar, or an altar, to mark the concrete physical spot where he sensed a special connection between heaven and earth, so that he can find his way back. Every temple, every shrine, every mosque, and every holy site is understood to be a ladder between heaven and earth, with the angels of God ascending and descending. Each is a special place where one can go to pray.

But there's a second kind of church that has nothing to do with buildings or holy sites. This is the church that Jesus reveals to the Samaritan woman in the Gospel of John (John 4:4–26). Most of us are familiar with the dialogue Jesus has with this woman. In their conversation she confesses a certain confusion regarding where to worship. She tells Jesus that she lives in a world that disagrees about where the real ladder between heaven and earth is to be found: the Jews tell her that the authentic place to worship is the temple in Jerusalem, but her own community, the Samaritans, tell her that the proper place to worship is Mount Gerizim. So what does Jesus say to her regarding which is the right place to worship?

Jesus tells her that she need not necessarily worship at either of those sites. Rather, the real temple, the real sacred place, the real privileged place where a ladder runs between heaven and earth, upon which angels ascend and descend, is inside her. The real church is not always a building or a holy site, but a place of conscience and spirit inside a person, accessible to them without their having to travel to the Holy Land, Rome, London, Salt Lake City, Mecca, Lourdes, or the neighborhood church. The ladder upon which angels ascend and descend between heaven and earth can be found everywhere: nature itself is a cathedral and, inside each of us, there's a church.

Thus there are two real churches given to us by God: one is outside us, physical and concrete; the other is inside us, spiritual and amorphous. Ideally, of course, a healthy sense of church would have us all worshipping deeply at both places, outside in our church buildings and inside in our hearts and consciences. Unfortunately, that isn't always the case. Huge ecclesial tensions exist today within all major religions and within all Christian denominations, between those who define church primarily or exclusively by one's active participation inside a church building (If you aren't coming to church, you aren't a real believer!) and those who define church, however unconsciously, as sincerity and worship within conscience and spirit (I'm spiritual but not religious!).

Both are right, both are wrong, and both need to widen their understanding of church. God gave us both churches, and both are vital. I know people, not least some very good male friends, who struggle with spiritual interiority. They grasp the meaning of church buildings, holy sites, and church structures, and these genuinely ground their religious lives. They can relate to the church as a building and as an institution that holds holy services; they can grasp Jacob's ladder there. Conversely, I know people, not least some very good female friends, who have a rich spiritual interiority but who struggle with the church as an institution, one that, to their mind, too easily and sometimes idolatrously privileges certain human organizations, sites, and persons as sine qua non avenues to heaven; they struggle to see Jacob's ladder inside such concrete, imperfect physicality.

Both need to learn from each other, and grasp more deeply the interrelationship of the two churches that God gave us.

Naming the Struggles with Faith Within Secularity

Sometimes the simple act of naming something can be immensely helpful. Before we can put a name on something we stand more helpless before its effects, not really knowing what's happening to us.

What are the major faith struggles of our time, within the more highly secularized parts of our world? There are ten that deserve particular attention:

1. The struggle with the atheism of our everyday consciousness—that is, the struggle to have a vital sense of God within a secular culture that, for good and bad, is the most powerful narcotic ever perpetrated on this planet—the struggle to be conscious of God outside church and explicit religious activity.

2. The struggle to live in torn, divided, and highly polarized communities, as wounded persons ourselves, and carry that tension without resentment and without giving it back in kind; the struggle inside our own wounded selves to be healers and peacemakers rather than contribute to the tension.

3. The struggle to live, love, and forgive beyond the infectious ideologies that we daily inhale—that is, the struggle for true sincerity, to genuinely know and follow our own hearts and minds beyond what is prescribed to us by the Right and the Left—the struggle to be neither liberal nor conservative but rather men and women of true compassion.

4. The struggle to carry our sexuality without undue frigidity and without irresponsibility; the struggle for a healthy sexuality that can both properly revere and properly delight in this great power; the struggle to carry our sexuality in such a way so as to radiate both chastity and passion.

5. The struggle for interiority and prayer inside a culture that in its thirst for informa-

tion and distraction constitutes a virtual conspiracy against depth and solitude, the eclipse of silence in our world; the struggle to move our eyes beyond our digital screens toward a deeper horizon.

6. The struggle to deal in a healthy way with "the dragon" of personal grandiosity, ambition, and pathological restlessness inside a culture that daily overstimulates them; the struggle to cope in a healthy way with both affirmation and rejection; the struggle inside a restless and overstimulated environment to habitually find the delicate balance between depression and inflation.

7. The struggle not to be motivated by paranoia, fear, narrowness, and overprotectionism in the face of terrorism and overpowering complexity; the struggle not to let our need for clarity and security trump compassion and truth.

8. The struggle with moral loneliness inside a religious, cultural, political, and moral diaspora; the struggle to find a soul mate who meets us and sleeps with us inside our moral center.

9. The struggle to link faith to justice; the

struggle to get a letter of reference from the poor, to institutionally connect the Gospels to the streets, to remain on the side of the poor.

10. The struggle for community and church; the struggle inside a culture of excessive individuality to find the healthy line between individuality and community, spirituality and ecclesiology; the struggle as adult children of the Enlightenment to be both mature and committed, spiritual and ecclesial.

What is the value in a list of this sort? It's important to name things and to name them properly; although, admittedly, simply naming a disease doesn't in and of itself bring about a cure. However, as James Hillman used to quip, "a symptom suffers most when it doesn't know where it belongs."

Working Through Five Hundred Years of Misunderstanding

"The heart has its reasons," says Blaise Pascal, the famous mathematician, physicist, and theologian, and sometimes those reasons have a long history.

I recently signed a card for a friend, a devout Baptist who was raised to have a suspicion of Roman Catholics. It's something he still struggles with—but don't we all! History eventually infects our DNA. Who of us is entirely free from suspicion of what is religiously different from our own beliefs? And what's the cure? Personal contact, friendship, and theological dialogue with those of other denominations and faiths do help to open our minds and hearts, but the fruit of centuries of bitter misunderstanding doesn't disappear so easily, especially when it's institutionally entrenched and nurtured as a prophetic protection of God and truth. In regard to Christians of other denominations there remains in most of us an emotional unease, an inability to see the other fully as one of our own.

And so in signing this card for my separated Christian friend, I wrote: "To a fellow Christian, a brother in the Body of Christ, a good friend, from whom I'm separated by 500 years of misunderstanding."

Five hundred years of misunderstanding, of separation, of suspicion, of defensiveness—that's not something easily overcome, especially when at its core sit issues about God, truth, and religion. Granted, there has been much positive progress made in the past fifty years, and many of the original, more blatant misunderstandings have been overcome. But the effects of the historical break within Christianity and the reaction to it are present today and are still seen everywhere, from high church offices, to debates within the academy of theology, to suspicions inside the popular mind.

Sadly, we've focused so much on our differences, when at the center, at the heart, we share the same essential faith, the same essential beliefs, the same basic moral codes, the same scriptures, the same belief in an afterlife, and the same fundamental tenet that intimacy with Jesus Christ is the aim of our faith. And today, not insignificantly, we also share the same prejudices and biases against us, whether these come from fundamentalists within other religions or overzealous, oversecularized, post-Christians within our own society. To someone looking at us from the outside, all the different Christian denominations look like a monolith, one faith, one church, a single religion, our differences far overshadowed by our commonality. Sadly, we tend not to see ourselves like this from within, where our differences, more often than not based upon a misunderstanding, are seen to dwarf our common discipleship.

Yet, the Epistle to the Ephesians tells us that, as Christians, we share *one Lord, one faith, one baptism, and one God who is Father of all of us* (Ephesians 4:5–6). At its most essential level, that's true of all of us as Christians, despite our denominational differences. We are one at our core.

Granted, there are some real differences among us, though most are in terms of how we understand certain aspects of the church and certain moral issues, rather than how we understand the deeper truths about the nature of God, the divinity of Christ, the gift of God's Word, the gift of the Eucharist, and the inalienable dignity and destiny of all human beings. Within the hierarchy of truth this essential core is what's most important, and on this essential core we essentially agree. That's the real basis of our common discipleship.

The ecclesial issues that divide us focus mostly on church authority, on ordination to ministry, on whether to emphasize word or sacrament, on how to understand the presence of Christ in the Eucharist, on the number of sacraments, on the place of sacramentals and devotions within discipleship, and on how the scriptures and tradition interplay with each other. In terms of moral issues, the issues that divide us are also the "hot-button" issues within our society as a whole: abortion, gay marriage, birth control, and the place of social justice within discipleship. But even on these, there's more commonality than difference among the churches.

Moreover, the differences on how we understand many of the ecclesial and moral issues that divide us today are more *temperamental* than *denominational;* that is, they tend to be more a question of one's theology than of one's denominational affiliation. Granted, classical denominational theology still factors in, but the divisions today regarding how we see certain ecclesial and moral issues—for example, ordination, gay marriage, abortion, social justice—are less a tension between Roman Catholics and Protestants and Evangelicals than between individuals who lean temperamentally and theologically in one direction rather than the other. It's perhaps too simplistic to paint this in terms of liberal versus conservative, but this much at least is true: the fault line on these issues today is becoming less denominational.

The earliest Christian creed contained a single line: *Jesus is Lord!* All Christians still agree on that, and so we remain brothers and sisters, separated only by five hundred years of misunderstanding.

CHAPTER EIGHT

Some Guidelines for the Long Haul

Simplify Your Spiritual Vocabulary

Around his seventy-fifth birthday, the Australian novelist Morris West wrote a series of autobiographical essays titled *A View from the Ridge*. In the prologue, he suggests that at age seventy-five you need to have only one word left in your spiritual vocabulary—"gratitude"—and that maturity is attained precisely at that moment when gratitude begins to drown out and cauterize the hurts in your life. As he describes it: "Life has served me as it serves everyone, sometimes well and sometimes ill, but I have learned to be grateful for the gift of it, for the love that began it and the other loves with which I have been so richly endowed."

I agree with West, though it is necessary to add that the

fruit of that maturity is forgiveness. Just as smoke follows fire, forgiveness follows gratitude. Gratitude ultimately undergirds and fuels all genuine virtue; it is the real basis of holiness and the source of love itself. And its major fruit is forgiveness. When we are grateful we more easily find the strength to forgive.

Moreover, just as gratitude undergirds genuine virtue, forgiveness undergirds genuine religion and morality. Thus, as we get older, we can trim our spiritual vocabulary down to three words: Forgive, forgive, forgive! To age into and then die with a forgiving heart is the ultimate moral and religious imperative. We shouldn't delude ourselves on this. All the dogmatic and moral purity in the world does little for us if our hearts are bitter and incapable of forgiveness.

We see this, for instance, in the sad figure of the older brother of the prodigal son. He stands before his father protesting that he has never wandered, that he has never been unfaithful, and that he has stayed home and done the family's work. But—and this is the issue—he stands outside his father's house, unable to enter into joy, celebration, the banquet, the dance. He's done everything right, but a bitter heart prevents him from entering his father's house just as much as the lustful wanderings of his younger brother took him out of that same house. Religious and moral fidelity, when not rooted inside gratitude and forgiveness, are far from enough. They can leave us just as much outside our father's house as sin and infidelity. As Jesus teaches forcefully in the Lord's Prayer, a nonnegotiable condition for going to heaven is forgiveness, especially our forgiving those who have hurt us.

But the struggle to forgive others is not easy and may never be trivialized or preached lightly. The struggle to forgive, I suspect, is our greatest psychological, moral, and religious struggle. It's not easy to forgive. Most everything inside us protests. When we have been wronged, when we have suffered an injustice, when someone or something has treated us unfairly, a thousand physical and psychological mechanisms inside us begin to clam up, shut down, freeze over, self-protect, and scream out in protest, anger, and rage. Forgiveness is not something we can simply will and make happen. The heart, as Pascal once said, has its reasons. It also has its rhythms, its paranoia, its cold bitter spots, and its need to seal itself off from whatever has wounded it.

Moreover, all of us have been wounded. No one comes to adulthood with his or her heart fully intact. In ways small or traumatic, we have all been treated unjustly, violated, hurt, ignored, not properly honored, and unfairly cast aside. We all carry wounds and, with those wounds, we all carry some anger, some bitterness, and some areas within which we have not forgiven.

The strength of Henri Nouwen's greatest book, *The Return of the Prodigal Son,* was precisely to point out both the hidden cold places in our hearts and the mammoth struggle needed to bring warmth and forgiveness to those places. So much of the lightness or heaviness in our hearts, nearly every nuance of our mood, is unconsciously dictated by either the forgiveness or the unforgiveness inside us. Forgiveness is the deep secret to joy. It is also the ultimate imperative.

In his review of Frank McCourt's book *Angela's Ashes*, theologian and novelist Andrew Greeley praised McCourt for being brilliant, but challenged him for being unforgiving with words to this effect: Granted, your life has been unfair. Your father was an alcoholic, your mother didn't protect you from the effects of that, you grew up in dire poverty, and you suffered a series of mini-injustices under the Irish social services, the Irish church, the Irish educational system, and the Irish weather! So, let me give you some advice: Before you die, forgive! Forgive your father for being an alcoholic, forgive your mother for not protecting you, forgive the church for the ways it failed you, forgive Ireland for the poverty, rain, and bad teachers it inflicted on you, forgive yourself for the failures of your own life, and then forgive God because life isn't fair . . . so that you don't die an angry and bitter man because that's really the ultimate moral imperative.

The First Words Out of Jesus's Mouth

We don't realize how much paranoia we carry within ourselves. A lot of things tend to ruin our day.

I went to a meeting recently and for most of it felt warm and friendly toward my colleagues, and positive about all that was happening. I was in good spirits, generative, and looking for places to be helpful. Then, shortly before the meeting ended, one of my colleagues made a biting comment that struck me as bitter and unfair. Immediately, a series of doors began to close inside me. My warmth and empathy quickly turned into hardness and anger, and I struggled not to obsess about the incident. Moreover, the feelings didn't pass quickly. For several days a coldness and paranoia lingered inside me, and I avoided any contact with the man who had made the negative comments while I stewed in my negativity.

Time and prayer eventually did their healing, a healthier perspective returned, and the doors that had slammed shut at that meeting opened again and metanoia replaced my paranoia.

It's significant that the first word out of Jesus's mouth in the Synoptic Gospels is "metanoia." Jesus begins his ministry with these words: "Repent [metanoia] and believe in the good news." That is a capsule summary of his entire message. But how does one repent?

Our English translations of the Gospels don't do justice to what Jesus is saying here. They translate "metanoia" with the word "repent." But, for us, the word "repent" has different connotations from what Jesus intended. In English, repentance implies that we have done something wrong and must regretfully disavow ourselves of that action and begin to live in a new way. The biblical word has much wider connotations.

"Metanoia" comes from two Greek words: *meta*, meaning "above," and *nous*, meaning "mind." Metanoia invites us to move above our normal instincts, into a bigger mind, into a mind that rises above the proclivity for self-interest and self-protection that so frequently triggers feelings of bitterness, negativity, and lack of empathy inside us. Metanoia invites us to meet all situations, however unfair they may seem, with understanding and an empathic heart. Moreover, metanoia stands in contrast to paranoia. In essence, metanoia is "nonparanoia," so Jesus's opening words in the Synoptic Gospels might be better rendered: "Be unparanoid and believe that it is good news. Live in trust!"

In *With Open Hands*, a small but deeply insightful book, Henri Nouwen perfectly describes the difference between metanoia and paranoia. He suggests that there are two fundamental postures with which we can go through life. We can, he says, go through life in the posture of paranoia. The posture of paranoia is symbolized by a closed fist, a protective stance, habitual suspicion and distrust. Paranoia makes us feel that we forever need to protect ourselves from unfairness, that others will hurt us if we show any vulnerability, and that we need to assert our strength and talents to impress others. Paranoia quickly turns warmth into cold, understanding into suspicion, and generosity into self-protection.

The posture of metanoia, on the other hand, is seen in Jesus on the cross: he is exposed and vulnerable, his arms spread in a gesture of embrace, and his hands open, with nails through them. That is the antithesis of paranoia, in which our inner doors of warmth, empathy, and trust spontaneously slam shut whenever we perceive a threat. Metanoia—the metamind, the bigger heart—never closes those doors.

Some of the early church fathers suggested that all of us have two minds and two hearts. For them, each of us has a big mind and a big heart. That's the saint in us, the image and likeness of God inside us, the warm, generative, and empathic part of us. All of us harbor a true greatness within. But within each of us is also a petty mind and a petty heart. That's the narcissistic part of us, the wounded part, the paranoid part that turns self-protective and immediately begins to close the doors of warmth and trust whenever we appear threatened. Such is our inner complexity. We are both bighearted and petty, open-minded and bigoted, trusting and suspicious, saint and narcissist, generous and hoarding, warm and cold. Everything depends upon which heart and which mind we are linked to and operating out of at any given moment. One minute we are willing to die for others, a minute later we would see them dead; one minute we want to give ourselves over in love, a minute later we want to use our gifts to show our superiority over others. Metanoia and paranoia vie for our hearts.

Jesus, in his message and his person, invites us to metanoia, to move toward and stay within our big minds and big hearts, so that in the face of a stinging remark our inner doors of warmth and trust do not close.

Carrying Tension So as to Take It Out of the Community

One of the things we're invited to do as adult Christians is to help "take away the sins of the world," as Jesus did. But how do we do this?

Jesus "took away the sins of the world" not by some magic act but by holding, carrying, purifying, and transforming tension. He did this by taking in the bitterness, anger, jealousy, hatred, slander, and every other kind of cancerous negativity within human community, and not giving it back in kind.

In essence, Jesus did this by acting like a purifier, a water filter of sorts: He took in hatred, held it, transformed it, and gave back love; he took in bitterness, held it, transformed it, and gave back graciousness; he took in curses, held them, transformed them, and gave back blessings; and he took in murder, held it, transformed it, and gave back forgiveness. Jesus resisted the instinct to give back in kind—hatred for hatred, curses for curses, jealousy for jealousy, murder for murder. He held and transformed these things rather than simply retransmit them.

And, in this, he wants imitation, not admiration. Christian discipleship invites us, like Jesus, to become a "lamb of God," a purifier who helps take tension out of our families, communities, friendship circles, churches, and workplaces by holding and transforming it rather than simply giving it back in kind.

But that's not easy. Jesus did this, but the Gospels say that he had to "sweat blood" to achieve it. To carry tension is to fill ourselves with tension and, as we know, this can be unbearable. We don't have God's strength and we aren't made of steel. As we try to carry tension for others, what do we do with our own tensions? How do we carry tension without becoming resentful and bitter? How do we carry another's cross without, however subtly, sending that person the bill?

As any health professional will tell you, tension wreaks havoc inside us physically and emotionally. Both high blood pressure and disappointment can kill you. But there are a few rules that can help you to cope.

First, carrying tension for others does not mean putting up with abuse or not confronting pathological or clinical dysfunction. To love someone, as we now know, does not mean accepting abuse in the name of love.

Second, we need to find healthy outlets to release our

own tensions. However, we should never download them on the same people for whom we are trying to carry them. For example, parents carry tension for their children, but, when frustrations build up, they should not angrily vent those dissatisfactions back on the kids themselves. Rather, they should deal with their own tensions away from the children, with each other and with friends, when the kids are in bed, over a bottle of wine. The same holds true for everyone: we should never vent our frustrations on the very people for whom we are trying to carry tension.

Finally, in order to deal with our mounting frustrations in the midst of carrying tension, we need to be connected to something (a hand, God, a creed, a perspective) beyond ourselves and the situation we're in.

The scriptures offer some wonderful images of being connected to something beyond ourselves when we are in crisis. For example, as Stephen was being stoned to death out of hatred and jealousy, he kept his "eyes raised to heaven." That's not so much a physical description of the event, as every artist knows, but a commentary on how Stephen kept himself from drowning in the spinning chaos that was assaulting him. He stayed connected to a person, a hand, a friendship, an affirmation, a perspective, and a divine power outside the madness.

A different metaphor is used to illustrate the same principle in the story of the three young men who were thrown into the blazing furnace in the book of Daniel. We're told that they walked around, right in the midst of the flames, untouched by the fire because they were singing sacred songs. Like Stephen, they sustained their love and faith amid bitter jealousy and hatred by staying connected to something outside the fiery forces that were consuming everyone else.

We need to contemplate that lesson. Like Jesus, we all find ourselves forever a part of families, communities, churches, friendships, and work circles that are filled with every kind of tension. Our natural temptation is always to simply give back in kind: jealousy for jealousy, gossip for gossip, anger for anger. But what our world really needs is for some women and men to step forward and help carry and purify this tension, to help take it away by transforming it inside themselves.

But it's not an easy process. Like Jesus, we will "sweat blood." So, as we volunteer to step into the fire, it's wise not to go in alone, but to stay connected to something—a hand, a friend, a creed, God—that will help sustain us in love and faith, right inside the madness and fire.

Pray, Even When You Don't Know How

"When we no longer know how to pray, the Spirit, in groans too deep for words, prays through us."

Saint Paul wrote those words and they contain both a stunning revelation and a wonderful consolation; namely, there is deep prayer happening inside us beyond our conscious awareness and independent of our deliberate efforts. What is this unconscious prayer? It is our deep innate desire, relentlessly on fire, forever somewhat frustrated, making itself felt through the groaning of our bodies and souls, silently begging the very energies of the universe, not least God himself, to let it come to consummation.

Allow me an analogy: Some years ago, a friend of mine bought a house that had sat empty and abandoned for a number of years. The surface of the driveway was cracked and a bamboo plant, now several feet high, had grown up through the pavement. My friend cut down the bamboo tree, chopped down several feet into its roots to try to destroy them, poured a chemical poison into the root system in hopes of killing whatever was left, packed some gravel over the spot, and paved over the top with a thick layer of concrete. But the little tree was not so easily thwarted. Two years later, the pavement began to heave as the bamboo plant again began to assert itself. Its powerful life force was still blindly pushing outward and upward, cement blockage notwithstanding.

Life, all life, has powerful inner pressures and is not easily thwarted. It pushes relentlessly and blindly toward its own ends, irrespective of resistance. Sometimes resistance does kill it. There are, as the saying goes, storms we cannot weather. But we do weather most of what life throws at us and our deep life principle remains strong and robust, even as on the surface the frustrations we have experienced and the dreams in us that have been shamed slowly muzzle us into a mute despair so that our prayer lives begin to express less and less of what we are actually feeling.

But it is through that very frustration that the spirit prays, darkly, silently, in groans too deep for words. In our striving, our yearning, our broken dreams, our tears, in the daydreams we escape into, and even in our sexual desire, the spirit of God prays through us, as does our soul, our life principle. Like the life forces innate in that bamboo plant, powerful forces are blindly working inside us too, pushing us outward and upward to eventually throw off whatever cement lies on top of us. This is true, of course, also of our joys. The spirit also prays through our gratitude, both when we express it consciously and even when we only sense it unconsciously.

Our deepest prayers are mostly not those we express in our churches and private oratories. Our deepest prayers are spoken in our silent gratitude and silent tears. The person praising God's name ecstatically and the person bitterly cursing God's name in anger are, in radically different ways of groaning, both praying.

There are many lessons to be drawn from this. First, we can learn to forgive life a little more for its frustrations and we can learn to give ourselves permission to be more patient with life and with ourselves. Who of us does not lament that the pressures and frustrations of life keep us from fully enjoying life's pleasures, from smelling the flowers, from being more present to family, from celebrating with friends, from peaceful solitude, and from deeper prayer? So we are forever making resolutions to slow down, to find a quiet space inside our pressured lives in which to pray. But, after failing over and over again, we eventually despair of finding a quiet, contemplative space for prayer in our lives. Although we need to continue to search for that, we can already live with the consolation that, deep down, our very frustration in not being able to find that quiet space is already a prayer. In the groans of our inadequacy the spirit is already praying through our bodies and souls in a way deeper than words.

One of the oldest, classical definitions of prayer defines it this way: prayer is lifting heart and mind to God. Too often in our efforts to pray formally, both communally and privately, we fail to do that—namely, to actually lift our hearts and minds to God. Why? Because what is really in our hearts and minds, alongside our gratitude and more gracious thoughts, is not something we generally connect with prayer at all. Our frustrations, bitterness, jealousies, lusts, curses, sloth, and quiet despair are usually understood to be the very antithesis of prayer, something to be overcome in order to pray.

But a deeper thing is happening under the surface: our frustration, longing, lust, jealousy, and escapist daydreams, things we are ashamed to take to prayer, are in fact already lifting our hearts and minds to God in more honest ways than we ever do consciously.

Remember That You Are Safe, Even in Death

As a priest, I have, a number of times, had to preside at the funeral of someone who died young, as the result of illness, accident, or suicide. Such a funeral is always doubly sad. I remember one in particular: A high school student had died in a car accident. The church was overpacked with his grieving family, friends, and classmates. His mother, still a young woman herself, was in the front pew, heavy with grief about her loss, but clearly weighed down too with anxiety for her child. After all, he was still just a boy, still in need of someone to take care of him, still needing a mother. She sensed how dying so young had in effect orphaned him.

There aren't many words that are helpful in a situation like this, but the few that we have say what needs to be said—even if on that day, when death is still so raw, they don't yet bring much emotional consolation. What's to be said in the face of a death like this? Simply that this young boy is now in more loving, more tender, gentler, and safer hands than ours, that there's a mother on the other side to receive him and give him the nurturing he still needs, just as there was one on this side when he was born. No one is born except into a mother's arms. That's an image we need to keep before us in order to imagine death in a healthier way.

What, more precisely, is the image? Few images are as primal, and as tender, as that of a mother holding and cradling her newborn baby. Indeed, the words of the most renowned Christmas carol of all time, "Silent Night," were inspired by precisely this image. Joseph Mohr, a young priest in Germany, had gone out to a cottage in the woods on the afternoon of Christmas Eve to baptize a newborn baby. As he left the cottage, the baby was asleep in its mother's lap. He was so taken with that image, with the depth and peace it incarnated, that, immediately upon returning to his rectory, he penned the famous lines of "Silent Night." His choir director, Franz Gruber, put some guitar chords to those words and froze them in our minds forever. The ultimate archetypal image of peace, safety, and security is that of a newborn sleeping in his mother's arms. Moreover, when a baby is born, it's not just the mother who's eager to hold and cradle it. Most everyone else is too.

Perhaps no image then is as apt, as powerful, as consoling, and as accurate in terms of picturing what happens to us when we die and awake to eternal life as is the image of a mother holding and cradling her newborn child. When we die, we die into the arms of God and surely we're received with as much love, gentleness, and tenderness as we were received in the arms of our mothers at birth. Moreover, surely we are even safer there than we were when we were born here on earth. I suspect too that more than a few of the saints will be hovering around, wanting their chance to cuddle the new baby. And so it's okay if we die before we're ready, still in need of nurturing, still needing someone to help take care of us, still needing a mother. We're in safe, nurturing, gentle hands.

That can be deeply consoling because death renders every one of us an orphan and, daily, there are people dying young, unexpectedly, less than fully ready, still in need of care themselves. All of us die still needing a mother. But we have the assurance of our faith that we will be born into safer and more nurturing hands than our own.

Our Unfinished Symphony—Living with Regrets

In a recent book, *The Invention of Wings*, Sue Monk Kidd presents us with a deeply conflicted heroine, Sarah, a highly sensitive woman who grows up the daughter of a slave owner and a child of privilege. But Sarah's moral sensitivity soon trumps her sense of privilege and she makes a series of hard choices to distance herself from both slavery and privilege.

Perhaps the most difficult among those hard choices is refusing an offer of marriage. Sarah badly wants marriage, motherhood, and children, but when the man she has loved for years finally proposes, there are things inside her that she won't compromise and she ends up saying no. What was her hesitancy?

When her suitor, Israel, finally proposes, Sarah asks him whether, inside their marriage, she could still pursue her dream to become a Quaker minister. Israel, a man of his time who could only grasp a woman's role as that of wife and mother, is frank in his reply. For him, that could not be a possibility. Sarah immediately intuits the implications of that answer: "It was his way of telling me. I could not have him and myself both." Her suitor then further aggravates the situation by suggesting that her desire to become a minister is simply a compensation, a second best, for not being married. She turns down his offer.

But a renunciation does not cease being painful just because it has been made for a noble reason. Throughout her life, Sarah often feels an acute regret for her choice, for having her principles trump her heart. However, she eventually makes peace with her regrets. Feeling the bitterness of her loss more acutely on the day of her sister's wedding, she shares with her sister how "I longed for it [marriage] in that excruciating way one has of romanticizing the life she didn't choose. But sitting here now, I knew if I'd accepted Israel's proposal, I would've regretted that, too. I'd chosen the regret I could live with best, that's all. I'd chosen the life I belonged to."

There will always be regrets in our lives, deep regrets. Thomas Aquinas suggests that every choice is also a renunciation. For this reason, we find it so difficult to make hard choices, particularly as these pertain to any type of permanent commitment. We want the right things, but we do not want to forgo other things. We want it all!

But we can't have it all, none of us, no matter how full of talent, energy, and opportunity we are; and sometimes it takes us a long time to properly understand why. At one point in Kidd's story, Sarah, in her thirties, single, unemployed, mainly alienated from her own family, frustrated by society's restrictions and her limited choices as a woman, is living as a guest with a woman friend, Lucretia, a Quaker minister. One evening, while sitting with Lucretia and lamenting the limits of her life, Sarah asks, "Why would God plant such deep yearnings in us . . . if they only come to nothing? It was more of a sigh than a question," but Lucretia replies, "God fills us with all sorts of yearnings that go against the grain of the world—but the fact those yearnings often come to nothing, well, I doubt that's God's doing. . . . I think we know that's men's doing."

For Lucretia, if the world were only fair, we'd have no broken dreams. She's partly right; much of what's wrong on this planet is our doing. But our frustrations ultimately tap into a deeper, less culpable root, the inadequacy of life itself. On this side of eternity, life is not whole. On this side of eternity, we are not whole. On this side of eternity, nothing is whole. In the words of Karl Rahner, "In the torment of the insufficiency of everything attainable we ultimately learn that in this life all symphonies remain unfinished."

This has many implications, not least the simple (though not easily digestible) fact that we can't have it all or do it all. Our lives have very real limits and we need to stop crucifying what we have and what we have achieved by comparing it to what we haven't got and what we haven't achieved. Despite the current myth to the contrary, no one gets it all! Most of us, I suspect, can relate to some of these regrets: I've raised my children well, but now I will never go anywhere professionally. I'm very successful at work, but I am less successful as a husband and father. I never married for the wrong reasons, but now I am single and alone. I've sacrificed ordinary life for an ideal, but now I fiercely miss what I've had to give up. Or, like Sue Monk Kidd's Sarah: I've never compromised my principles, but that has brought a brutal loneliness into my life.

It's never a matter of living with regrets or without them. Everyone has regrets. Hopefully, though, we've chosen the regrets we can live with best.

And in the End All Will Be Well

Pierre Teilhard de Chardin was once making a presentation to a group of scientists, some of whom were agnostics and atheists. Teilhard, a man who guided his life by a vision of Christian hope, was presenting a vision wherein all of history would eventually culminate in certain salvific harmony within which everything, cosmic and human, would unite in one communion of love and peace.

Not everyone in his audience shared his vision, but it's a vision of hope inherent in all authentic religious traditions, not least in Christianity. As the famed mystic Julian of Norwich once put it: "all shall be well, and all shall be well, and all manner of being shall be well." This is true for all of us, no matter our human deficiencies, our moral inadequacies, or the short straws we might draw in this life. Our story will eventually have a happy ending. That's a faith statement not based upon either wishful thinking or natural optimism, but upon a promise from God. This belief that ultimately all of us and everything in the world are safe lies at the base of every major religious tradition. Thus, we can live free of fear and let our lives flourish.

And it's for this reason that in our search for life, meaning, happiness, and faith, we can find incalculable help by delving into the deep wells of religious tradition. More than any ideology in the world, they can provide us with the road maps, the GPS, the vision, and the hope we need for our journey.

Speaking personally, as I age and my faith and spirituality mature, each year I find myself living with less fear, particularly of God, the future, my aging, my own death, and what happens after death. It is a wonderful freedom that comes with age—and with faith. All the great religious traditions, not least Christianity, assure us that we are in safer hands on the other side of this world than we are here—which should leave us with little to fear on this side because eventually all graves will be empty, including our own.

And so, as Oscar Wilde once put it: "Everything is going to be fine in the end. If it's not fine it's not the end."

ACKNOWLEDGMENTS

My gratitude goes out to many who were influential in bringing this book to light, but a few need to be named specially: Thanks to Gary Jansen at Image Books for suggesting that I write this book and then midwifing it to completion. Thanks to his editorial staff for their infinite patience with this digital immigrant who wasn't able always to negotiate through the electronic software within which they were speaking to me. Thanks to Alicia von Stamwitz for her editorial help and thanks to Tom and Ginger Kemmy who lent me their beach house as a wonderful space within which to finish the writing. Not least, thanks to all those who support me: my family, the faculty and students at Oblate School of Theology in San Antonio, Texas, and my religious community, the Missionary Oblates of Mary Immaculate, who cheerfully provide for me even as they endure my foibles.

Acknowledgments

A number of the sections in this book appeared previously as articles in various newspapers for which I write: the *Western Catholic Reporter* (Edmonton), the *Catholic Register* (Toronto), and the *Catholic Herald* (London), among others.

SACRED FIRE

A VISION FOR
A DEEPER HUMAN AND
CHRISTIAN MATURITY

RONALD ROLHEISER

DISCIPLESHIP AND THE STAGES OF OUR LIVES

What we choose to fight is so tiny!
What fights with us is so great!
If only we would let ourselves be dominated
as things do by some immense storm,
we would become strong too, and not need names.

—RAINER MARIA RILKE, "THE MAN WATCHING"

The Seasons of Our Life and Their Interface with Spirituality

The human soul is like a fine wine that needs to ferment in various barrels as it ages and mellows. The wisdom for this is written everywhere, in nature, in scripture, in spiritual traditions, and in what is best in human science. And that wisdom is generally learned in the crucible of struggle. Growing up and maturing is precisely a process of fermentation. It does not happen easily, without effort and without breakdown. But it happens almost despite us, because such is the effect of a conspiracy between God and nature to mellow the soul.

How does it happen? What are the various barrels within which we find ourselves fermenting? How is the soul mellowed within the crucible of struggle? We mature by meeting life, just as God and nature designed it, and accepting there the invitations that beckon us ever deeper into the heart of life itself. But that is a simple cliché, more easily said than done, because as we go through the seasons of our lives the challenges we meet there can just as easily embitter and harden the soul as mellow it.

So we need to be patient with one another and with ourselves. Maturation is a lifelong journey with different phases, human and spiritual. And it has many setbacks. What can be helpful is to have a grasp of the natural seasons of our lives and how these interface with a vision of Christian discipleship and its particular stages. What are the seasons of life and what are the stages of discipleship?

A parable might help set the stage: in his autobiography, the renowned writer Nikos Kazantzakis shares a conversation he once had with an old monk named Father Makários. Sitting with the saintly old man, Kazantzakis asked him: "Do you still wrestle with the devil, Father Makários?" The old monk reflected for a while and then replied: "Not any longer, my child. I have grown old now, and he has grown old with me. He doesn't have the strength. . . . I wrestle with God."

"With God!" exclaimed the astonished young writer. "And you hope to win?" "I hope to lose, my child," replied the old ascetic. "My bones remain with me still, and they continue to resist."[1]

The lesson here is that we struggle with different forces at various times in our lives. We are always struggling and doing battle with something, but the forces that beset us change with the years. When we are young and still trying to establish an identity, these forces are very much embedded in the chaotic, fiery energies of restlessness, wanderlust, sexuality, the quest for freedom, and the sheer hunger for experience. The struggle with these energies can be disorienting and overpowering, even though they are the engines that drive us and propel us into adult life. The process of growing up is rarely serene. It is a struggle, a wrestling match with every kind of untamed energy. Everyone has his or her own tale, usually involving a lot of painful restlessness and a few shameful humiliations, of the not-so-gentle passage from childhood to adulthood.

Moreover, it is not that these energies ever go dormant or disappear from inside us; other struggles just set in and begin to eclipse them. As we sort out more who we are, make permanent commitments, and take on more and more responsibilities, we soon find ourselves beset by a new set of struggles: disappointment, tiredness, boredom, frustration, resentment. Consciously and unconsciously, we begin to sense that the big dream for our lives is over, without its ever paying the huge dividends we expected. We become disappointed that there is not more, that we have not achieved more, and that we ourselves are not more, as we sense ourselves stuck with second best, reluctant to make our peace there. All those grandiose dreams, all that potential, all that energy, and what have we achieved? Most all of us can relate to Henry David Thoreau's famous line: "The youth gets together his materials to build a bridge to the moon, or, perchance, a palace or temple on the earth, and, at length, the middle-aged man concludes to build a woodshed with them."[2] And that is a comedown that is not easily digested.

Moreover, once the sheer pulse of life, so strong in us during our youth, begins to be tempered by the weight of our commitments and the grind of the years, more of our sensitivities begin to break through, and we sense more and more how we have been wounded and how life has not been fair to us. New demons then emerge: bitterness, anger, jealousy, and a sense of having been cheated.[3] Disappointment cools the fiery energies of our youth, and our enthusiasm for life begins to be tempered by bitterness and anger as we struggle to accept our limits and make peace with a life that now seems too small and unfair. Where we once struggled to properly control our energies, we now struggle to access them. Where we once struggled not to fall apart, we now struggle not to petrify. Where we once struggled with Eros, the god of passion, we now struggle with Lyssa, the goddess of anger. And where our sympathies once were with the prodigal son, they now are more with his older brother. As we age we begin more and more to struggle with God.

Someone once quipped that we spend the first half of our lives struggling with the sixth commandment (*Thou shalt not commit adultery*) and the second half of our lives struggling with the fifth commandment (*Thou shalt not kill*). That may be a simplification, but it is a fertile image. Indeed the famous parable of the prodigal son and his older brother can serve as a paradigm for this: the prodigal son, illustrating the first half of life, is very much caught up in the fiery energies of youth and is, metaphorically, struggling with the devil; the older brother, illustrating the second half of life, struggling instead with resentment, anger, and jealousy, is, metaphorically and in reality, wrestling with God.

The point of the example is not so much to name or pinpoint what particular things we need to struggle with during the different seasons of our lives, but that there are precisely different seasons in our lives, each with distinct challenges.